EBURY PRESS
DIRECTORS' DIARIES 2

Rakesh Anand Bakshi is a scriptwriter and the author of *Directors' Diaries: The Road to Their First Film* and *Let's Talk on Air: Conversations with Radio Presenters*. He is an aspiring director and actor, and a swimming, cycling and gym enthusiast. Rakesh runs Bicycle Angels, a non-profit social initiative supported by friends that gives bicycles and wheelchairs to the underprivileged and teaches the visually impaired how to use a computer. He also co-founded, with Kanika Kedia, I Adore You Diaries, which creates personalized diaries. He authors a blog, Beautiful Bicycles Beautiful People, on cyclists, their rides and stories.

ADVANCE PRAISE FOR THE BOOK

'A must read for all, just like Volume 1. It gives an incredible insight into the director's mind and the world of movies. The anecdotes will greatly help future generation of film-makers understand the journey and complexities that one must go through while making a career as a director'—**Vishal Bhardwaj**

'Every film-maker has a struggle and a journey that is unique to him/her. I loved reading how the directors in this book made their first film, because those are most special. These stories are not only inspirational, but also cinematic in their telling . . . each one can be a biopic on its own!'—**Farah Khan**

'Inspiration for the dreamy-eyed young Indian who wants to make it to the film industry one day'—**Imtiaz Ali**

'Rakesh Bakshi's second edition of *Directors' Diaries* not only puts the spotlight on film-makers but also their cinematographers, make-up artists, sound designers and even the spot boy. So learn on!'—**Ashutosh Gowariker**

'These probing conversations reveal more about the mystery of cinema than many how-to books. A must if you love the medium'—**Baradwaj Rangan**

'A superpower of films, India, now has another wonderful guide for future film-makers and cinephiles, the second volume of *Directors' Diaries* charting "Their Path to Film-making"—full of gems, a collection of "Conversations With Eminent Film-makers", also an entertaining and enlightening read for the general audience'—**Prof. Karl Bardosh, associate arts professor, New York University**

DIRECTORS' DIARIES 2

Conversations with *Film-makers*
Their Path to Film-making

RAKESH ANAND BAKSHI

EBURY
PRESS

An imprint of Penguin Random House

EBURY PRESS

USA | Canada | UK | Ireland | Australia
New Zealand | India | South Africa | China | Singapore

Ebury Press is part of the Penguin Random House group of companies
whose addresses can be found at global.penguinrandomhouse.com

Published by Penguin Random House India Pvt. Ltd
4th Floor, Capital Tower 1, MG Road,
Gurugram 122 002, Haryana, India

First published in Ebury Press by Penguin Random House India 2019

ISBN 9780143449089

Typeset in Adobe Garamond Pro by Manipal Technologies Limited, Manipal

Printed at Repro India Limited

www.penguin.co.in

To those who were there, and are not,
and to those who were there, and are:
my mother, Kamla Mohan,
my father, Anand Prakash Bakshi,
my brother, Rajesh (Gogi), and
my sisters, Suman (Pappi) and Kavita (Rani).
I love you all, even though I may not always express it.

The author with his father at Mahabaleshwar Lake, during their
annual summer holiday

CONTENTS

FOREWORD

The director, auteur, or technician is responsible for everything in the film-making process—from writing, costume, make-up, working with actors, discussions with the director of photography (DOP) to getting the sound levels and score right, working on the pace of a scene and its look with the editors. All this before they have even shouted 'Action!' What I have mentioned is by no means exhaustive, but it gives you a sense of the magnitude of a director's efforts. The people who manage this with aplomb are masters of a very special skill.

I have been in the world of film-making for over five decades and have been a director for over forty years. During this time, I have heard every possible cliché and comment about directing and what it takes to be a successful one. Most of these encompass only a fraction of the real story.

As a professional, this is something I took time to learn. Fortunately, I had good teachers and mentors and I am sincerely grateful to them. That is why I decided to start a film-making school, as I firmly believe that this is a skill and a craft that can and must be taught. Today, young film-makers have so much imagination that needs guidance and nurturing so they can go on and have careers that will last the rest of their lives. That is how a director really learns their craft. By making films. Many films, with many stories, for many lifetimes.

I was part of the first volume of this wonderful compilation of stories. I believe both these volumes are a truly wonderful resource for young film-makers. It is therefore my pleasure to write the foreword to the second volume of this anthology, as every director has a different method and you can always learn something from each person. I am sure I will learn a lot too about this most compelling of arts.

Rakesh Anand Bakshi did a great job writing *Directors' Diaries: The Road to Their First Film*, and my personal congratulations and best wishes to him for the great success of yet another invaluable volume.

Subhash Ghai,
Chairman,
Whistling Woods International Institute of Film,
Communication and Creative Arts, Mumbai

AUTHOR'S NOTE

This anthology is a tribute to my father, Anand Bakshi (Anand Prakash Bakshi), who wrote nearly 3300 songs for 623 Hindi and Punjabi films from 1956 to 2002. His first poem was published on 25 March 1950 in the Indian Army publication *Sainik Samachar*. The publication of his poem and the birth of his first child, a girl (his grandmother had told him that a girl child brought good luck to the family) gave him the required confidence to try his luck in Hindi cinema as a lyricist. So, he left the army and moved to Bambai (Bombay/Mumbai).

> *Girengi bijliyan kab tak, jalenge aashiya kab tak*
> *Khilaf aehale chaman ke, tu rahege aasman kab tak.*
>
> *Satayega, rulayega, jaleyega jahaan kab tak,*
> *Zameeron, zaiheno, jism, jaan se, niklega dhuan kab tak.*
>
> *Nizam-e-gulistaan, ehl-e-gulistan hi sambhalenge,*
> *Teri manmaniyan, teri hukumat, baaghban kab tak.*
>
> *Hamari badnaseebi ki aakhir koi hadh bhi hogi,*
> *Rahoge hum par tum, na meherban, eh meherbaan, kab tak.*
>
> *Meri aankhen barasti hain musalsal hijr mein Bakhshi,*
> *Mukabil inke barsengi bhala ye badliyan, kab tak.*

'You got to make your own breaks!
You got to write your own biography.'

—Anand Bakshi

INTRODUCTION

If, as Ellen Terry says, 'Drama is the child of theatre', the film director is the child of cinema.

Quoting from the introduction to HarperCollins India's Volume 1 of *Directors' Diaries*: 'A thought that has always fascinated me is that our past makes our present; our present makes our future.' Sometime in 2002, I read in a book that David Lean, the English director known for films like *Lawrence of Arabia* and *Dr Zhivago*, used to be a tea boy. He then became a messenger, then an editor and finally a director. It made me wonder about Lean's life and I thought that if he hadn't started out as a tea boy, he perhaps wouldn't have become a director. Maybe he would not have discovered his love for films. I became interested in his life and the detours it must have taken to bring him where he was supposed to be. What did he do before he became a tea boy? What other jobs did he have before he became an editor? What sort of friends did he have? What films did he watch and what books did he read? What determined the course of his life? Such thoughts, amongst other as significant reasons, led to two volumes of this book.

Volume 1 of this anthology, published in 2015, featured Subhash Ghai, Imtiaz Ali, Farah Khan, Mahesh Bhatt, Vishal Bhardwaj, Ashutosh Gowariker, Anurag Basu, Zoya Akhtar, Tigmanshu Dhulia, Santosh Sivan, Prakash Jha, and Art Director/ Production Designer Nitin C. Desai; and cinematographers who had worked with these directors: Ravi Varman, Mahesh Aney, Manikandan Velayutham, Natarajan Subramaniam, Sachin Krishna,

Kabir Lal, Ranjan Palit and Aseem Mishra; and Production Designer and Art Director Nitin Desai. I had conversations with nearly thirty film-makers but could publish only twelve in Volume 1. This volume features directors we could not publish in the earlier one.

When I was an assistant director on various films in the period from 1999 to 2005, the first 'friends' I made from amongst the film crew were a spot boy, a make-up artist, a sound designer and an art director. They made me feel at ease on the film set as I was intimidated by the large number of people present, many of them super successful in their professions. In this second volume, I have decided to feature an eminent sound designer and audiographer, Rakesh Ranjan; make-up designer Vikram Gaikwad; and art director and spot boy Salim Shaikh aka Action, along with the directors. Many people think that a spot boy is the lowest rung in the hierarchy of a film set; however, I think spot boys, light men and the art director's crew lay the foundation for others to work on. Spot boys, too, are film-makers.

Shyam Benegal once said, 'A good spot boy is one who understands the nature of film production and anticipates, on the spot, the requirement for one thing or another even before the production or direction department asks for it. [. . .] My spot boy Kasim, who worked on many films with me, lived up to that.'

As for some of the reactions I received from the directors during and after our conversations for this book, one director said that it made him realize why he came to this profession in the first place. Some said they got to know things about themselves they had not realized earlier. One said it helped her discover more about herself.

Another thing I learnt during my years as an assistant director was that there is no one way to direct a film or write a script or direct actors. This book and its directors' opinions are not gospel truths or advice—they are opinions, and significant ones at that. Every director can have their own 'laws' about the art or skill of directing; however, nothing is set in stone. Their rules, if any, will evolve with their own evolution. I like to think that film direction as a profession is a matter of opinion. If convictions can change with experiences, opinions certainly can.

After learning so much about film-making from books and other sources, and meeting more than thirty directors over the last six years, I've realized that I know very little about film-making. So, ignorance of the craft will remain our companion throughout the film-making journey.

Directors' Diaries 2 is not addressed to prospective film-makers only, but also to enthusiastic filmgoers, cinema students and book lovers. Thank you for joining us on this journey. If our book can, in any way, stimulate thought and enrich creativity, making your understanding of the art and craft of films and life more fulfilling, we will be amply rewarded. Be inspired. Stay inspired. Stay loved.

THE DIRECTORS

ABHISHEK CHAUBEY

*'Things are going to get much harder before they become easier.
To survive that, you need to keep your heart, mind and soul where
they belong. Rooted together, they make a great anchor for our
ship to sustain the storms that life invariably brings upon us all.'*

FILMOGRAPHY

Ishqiya (2010); *Dedh Ishqiya* (2014); *Udta Punjab* (2016);
Sonchiriya (2019)

SNEAK PEEK

Abhishek was born in Faizabad, Uttar Pradesh, and grew up in
Patna, Ranchi and Jamshedpur till his early teens, as his father
had a transferrable bank job. He joined a boarding school in
Hyderabad in 1993 and attended college in New Delhi, graduating
in English literature. During his third year in college, he joined a
theatre group, Act One, but had no ambition of becoming a film
director; he simply enjoyed being an actor. Later, he decided to
move to Mumbai and joined the film and TV course at Xavier's
Institute of Communications in 1999. He worked as an extra in
a TVC commercial for Raymond pants, landing the role because
of his height (he is 6'1"), and later as a production assistant in a
TVC production house. His first job was as an assistant director
in *Shararat* (2002).

Soon, he was recommended by a friend (and co-producer of the proposed film *Makdee*), Sanjay Routray, to meet Vishal Bhardwaj, then an established composer making his first feature film. Bhardwaj was looking for assistants. Abhishek worked as an associate director with him on *Makdee* (2002); he began as a co-writer with Bhardwaj on *Blue Umbrella* (2005) and *Omkara* (2006). Since his first job as an assistant director in 2002 to his first foray as film director, it took eight long years.

MY TAKE

I met Abhishek for the first time at Whistling Woods International Film School during its annual event 'Celebrate Cinema'. Meghna Puri, the president of the school, introduced me to him. I was carrying a copy of *Directors' Diaries* and gifted it to him.

After seeing his first two films back-to-back, I thought they were about the pursuit of love at all costs. One of the many things I liked about his first three films was that they were shot in real locations. No sets. It rooted me to the narrative. And two of my favourite moments from his three films so far were from *Udta Punjab*. Mary Jane, the village girl played by Alia Bhatt, has been kidnapped and repeatedly drugged and gang-raped while she is held captive over many days. Holed up in a dingy room, she zones out of the trauma by looking out of the only window in that dark hellhole. Every time she is raped, before becoming unconscious as the drugs are injected into her, she fixes her progressively hazy gaze at a holiday destination billboard on the road in the distance. The billboard advertises good times in Goa, but for her it's a sign that all the suffering and torture will pass; a better life awaits her in the near future. I thought every one of us carries a cross, but not many of us keep such a window of hope open in our minds.

Another great moment from the same film has Tommy Singh, the star singer played by Shahid Kapoor, reaching the apogee of his immoral and irresponsible existence, and wanting to commit suicide. Tommy Singh proposes to Mary Jane that they should commit suicide together. Mary Jane lashes out at him, 'I am not a *lallu* [stupid] or *fuddu* [idiot] to commit suicide in spite of what I have suffered. What I have suffered is behind me, and my best times are yet to come, and I know they will and I want to live for those happy moments that definitely await me.' Long after I left the cinema hall, I pondered the subtle positivity in *Udta Punjab*. Many people said it was a sad, depressing and dark film; however, I felt the writer–director offered sunshine to those who can catch sight of the silver lining behind every dark cloud.

THE CONVERSATION

Rakesh Bakshi: *Thank you for being a part of this book. Which is your earliest memory of watching a film, and understanding that it's a movie that someone has made?*

Abhishek Chaubey (AC): It must have been sometime during the late 1980s or early '90s. I was living in Ranchi and didn't have any access to Hollywood at the time. We had a video cassette player and it was my main source of watching movies. I was watching a Hindi film featuring a jailbreak sequence. Though I knew zilch about film-making, and even less about jailbreaks, I felt the scene was illogical. In my head, I could even point out the technical fault with the scene. I felt strongly that there could be a better way of filming it. In hindsight, that was sort of an 'aha' moment for me, because it was my first realization that I understood something about film-making without knowing how movies were made! Now when I look back, I think I was actually staging that scene differently in my head.

What's the craziest thing you've done to watch a movie?

AC: My boarding school was in Kompally, a village back then, around 30–35 km from Hyderabad. I used to stay in the school hostel. I was in Class XI and part of the quiz team. Once, a contest was held in a school in the main city. The other members of the quiz team and I were serious about winning the contest. However, *Hum Hain Rahi Pyar Ke* (1993) released that same week. I desperately wanted to watch it but was not allowed to stay out late. The quiz contest was my way out. I deliberately fudged up the quiz to get disqualified in the very first written test round so I could go and watch *Hum Hain Rahi Pyar Ke*. Of course, I took my two teammates into confidence before doing so and they reluctantly agreed. The cinema hall was quite far from the school, so I ran for about 15–20 minutes to reach on time!

Which is the first film to have made a deep impression on you?

AC: *400 Blows* (1959) by François Truffaut influenced me a lot as a young adult. However, the film that remains embedded in my consciousness is Ingmar Bergman's *Persona* (1966). I saw it when I arrived in Mumbai in 2002. I have always been moved by how people identify themselves—their self-image and what they think the world thinks of them. *Persona* evokes these fascinating and moving thoughts in me. I can talk about its craft and art all day. This film made me more interested in film-making.

Did you have a plan B when you arrived in Mumbai looking for a job in the film industry?

AC: I never really had any opinion about a career when I was a young boy. It was only in my early teens that I decided to become a film director. I did not give myself a choice; I relied on my instincts. I belong to a middle-class family from a small town, where people believe that to be successful one has to pursue an MBA or IAS. However, I knew neither of these two or for that matter any private sector job would make me happy even if they made me successful. Since my teenage years, I felt happier watching movies. Everything in my immediate world would become brighter when I would be watching a film. I wanted to be like that all the time and wondered if I could become a part of the film world.

When was the first time you were drawn to learning film-making?

AC: Sometime in 1999, a friend of a friend recommended me for the job of an extra (actor), only because of my height, in a Raymond pants TVC commercial. Only my lower torso was visible in the ad! I clearly recall, while was I on the set of that shoot, that I could not make head or tail of what was going on [the film-making process]. I was just waiting to get done with it, as it paid well, and I needed the money. At that time, I was studying at Xavier Institute of Communications and had joined this year-long course only so my parents would allow me to stay in Mumbai! I was in love with someone back then and I pursued her and explored Bombay city life more than I pursued my film course and film dream! I then found a job as a production assistant on a TV show, thanks to my writing teacher at XIC and scriptwriter Urmi Juvekar. That was my first experience on a TV shooting floor. On this job, with the TV production company Magic Box, I began to understand how films are made, even though my responsibilities on the set were paltry. The show did not take off beyond the pilot episode. The episode director was Nishikant Kamath who later on went on to make the Marathi film *Dombivali Fast* (2005).

Actually, it was the process of writing that lit the first spark in me to take film-making seriously. During the XIC course, when I started writing short films for my graduation, I began to really enjoy the process. It was then that I started looking for a job in the film industry.

What was your first job in the movies, and what did you learn from it?

AC: My first job was as an assistant director for Gurudev Bhalla's *Shararat* (2002). I started off as an apprentice because I didn't really know anything about film-making and was not even from a film school. The only reason I could hold on to the job during pre-production was because I could write well. And I don't mean dialogue or scripts. I could draft administrative letters. Every time someone needed a letter to be typed out on a computer, whether for shooting permissions or booking a location, I was the person they approached! That was all. I didn't know what I was going to do on the set when the shooting started.

When we began filming, I was put in charge of the costumes. I worked in coordination with the dress department and managed to pick up on what was happening—on and off set. The good thing was that the film had a massive cast so I had a lot of work to do on the set and it helped me grow.

Once, after I had taken care of the actors' costumes and they were ready with make-up, I thought I could chill on the set. But when the director found out, I received a sound tongue-lashing. He taught me that once the costumes had been taken care of, I had to assist the other departments. Whether it was art direction, props or background action, an assistant's job was never over until after pack up.

Then ten days before the last schedule, the first assistant director fell ill and they could not find anyone to replace him. So I was promoted to first assistant and by the time the film was completed I had learnt the skills needed to run a set on my very first job! I have always been a soft-spoken person. I am still the same. But when I was made the first assistant, I had to crack the whip when needed. From being a follower of orders, I became a leader giving orders to his assistants. That experience taught me how to switch roles—from a quiet person to a leader. I learnt that about myself on my first job.

What job did you do post Shararat?

AC: I decided to make a documentary. It was about how society reacts to mental illness. A German TV channel showed interest in the fifteen-minute capsule that we had produced. But I was running out of money. I needed to pay rent and buy food. I got a call from a friend, Sanjay Routray (co-producer of *Makdee*), informing me that a music composer, Vishal Bhardwaj, was making his first feature film as a director and was looking for an assistant director. It was a three-month commitment and a low-budget film. I needed the money and went for it. That was the beginning of a relationship that contributed to my emergence as a director. Vishal-ji produced my first film as a director.

I must add that when I met him for the job, I was expecting him to ask me about film-making, setting up a team of assistants, etc. However, he asked me about my beliefs in superstitions, ghosts and spirits, and I had the job! *Makdee* was a story debunking the myth of ghosts and spirits. Also, it was on this film that I met Honey Trehan, who went on to become a casting director and is today my partner in MacGuffin Pictures. Together we co-produced *Death in the Gunj* (2016).

You are a writer–director. Did you read and/or write during your years in school and college? If yes, did that help you later as a writer and a director?

AC: Reading goes a long way if you want to become a film-maker. For example, if you want to make films, tell stories, reading is great because it teaches you how to structure a story. Every story needs to be revealed gradually; it needs to have layers; and one fundamental theme. That is what you get from being a regular reader. The learning of the craft happens organically. I developed a habit for reading while in Delhi. I was a literature student and started reading serious books. I had always been good at languages in school, though I wasn't a good student; I hated the idea of studying and mugging up something.

However, don't limit yourself to one thing, whether it's reading, writing, drawing or photography. I think you should also enjoy other forms, for example, music, which has always helped me visualize, just like reading did. I would shut my eyes listening to music in order to visualize better. Sometimes when I am writing an action scene, I try very hard to think of the background music that would play. That helps. Literature and music have both helped me as a writer–director.

Did your knowledge of literature and your experience in small towns in your formative years help you write the rural milieu of your first two films?

AC: Yes. *Ishqiya* and *Dedh Ishqiya* are both set in rural India, Gorakhpur. I know that part of the world well because my father is from Faizabad and my mother from Lucknow. I've spent a lot of time growing up in Purvanchal. I also instinctively understood the gender equations and dynamics in many rural families, through my interaction with my own extended family. Many of the women in our family wore the pants in the relationship. I built Vidya's, Huma's and Madhuri's characters around them.

As for the style and genre of the films I've made so far, if you look closely, they are sort of noir. And film noir is something that I understood early on by watching world cinema extensively and studying literature. Both these films are representative of that. Back in 2007, when I was thinking about my first film, I thought it would be quite trippy to take a classical Western noir idea and transpose it to a Purvanchali setting.

Was it hard to find a producer for your first film, considering noir and rural settings were not popular film concepts back then?

AC: Not really. But only because my first producers, Vishal-ji and Shemaroo, were already familiar with me. I was the associate director and co-writer of *Omkara*, which they had produced. So, they had seen me work on the sets and during the production of *Omkara*. Shemaroo offered that if I write a film, they would produce it. And Vishal-ji was already pushing me to direct a film that he would be willing to produce. So they believed in my vision when I presented them my script.

However, it was not all plain sailing. It took me a year to crack the script. And it was one of the toughest periods of my life. That one year was terrible, but I was determined to make it right. We reached a point where Vishal-ji said it was my call alone whether I wanted to make this film or not.

Once we had the script in place, we approached some top stars, but nobody was convinced. Many of them showed us the attitude—who the hell are you and what the hell is this film about and who is going to watch this because people watch a different kind of films—because those days urban films and those with NRIs as lead characters were doing well at the box office. No one but Naseeruddin Shah and Arshad Warsi saw value in our script and vision.

What kept you going in that period?

AC: The one thought that never left me during that period was that I had to become a director. Because that's all I had ever wanted to do in life. See, when you have refused everything that has come your way, before leaping to film-making, and it is you and only you who chose to become a film-maker, these in themselves become self-motivating factors. Then you do not need external motivation.

Having said that, [post *Omkara*] Vishal-ji's encouragement must have been a big factor too. For someone so successful to see some value in me mattered immensely. This at a time when some of my relatives and friends thought I was crazy to even think of becoming a director. But becoming a director was everything to me. My life depended on it.

Why did you feel your life depended on it?

AC: Because you want to make sense of your life, no? Your life needs to have some meaning for you. And for me, becoming a director would have added meaning and value to my existence.

After your first film as co-writer, you continued to write films. Why?

AC: Writing paid my bills. I knew it could be the stepping stone to direction. I worked as a co-writer on *The Blue Umbrella* (2005), *Omkara* and *Kaminey* (2009) before I pitched my script as a director to anyone. My first script became my first feature film.

Which other significant skills are required to become a film-maker?

AC: However hard or overwhelming it may seem to someone from outside, I think film direction is an Everyman's job. In the sense that, if you want to become a painter, you need to have a good hand, but you also need to have the right imagination and know-how to put your thoughts on drawing sheet. Likewise, if you want to be a singer, you need to have a good voice and you can train yourself to become a good singer. I think one has to be, as a film-maker, artistically inclined. What I mean is, one needs to read, watch and listen closely to be a film-maker.

As a film-maker, what you are really doing is telling a story. But understanding the story is a more important skill. It is a skill you may or may not have, but definitely a skill you need to/can develop.

I am still learning that skill, even as I am on my way to make my fourth film; I am still getting there; still making giant mistakes. Sometimes when you are young and want to make films, you get thrilled by an idea that you can visualize, which is great, but that is not what will make you a good film-maker. I think, what truly makes one a good film-maker is one's understanding of the story.

In Dedh Ishqiya, *there is a dialogue,* 'Talent ko will ka support chahiye *(Talent needs to be backed by a will).' What else is needed for that elusive first break as a director?*

AC: Tenacity is what I am really talking about. Grit! My mentor, Vishal-ji, has it and he infected me with it. I am highly optimistic.

Sooner than later everybody gets whatever they want as long as they don't lose their will or head by the time they reach their destination. I think this city, Mumbai, Bollywood, is like that. As in, it's very easy to lose your bearings. People can easily get frustrated and become edgy.

Also, this profession is entirely dependent on one's talent and personality and nothing else. Your educational qualifications don't matter. Self-doubt is always walking besides you.

In a world where many people are tempted to say yes to what they are being offered, because they need money or work, how important is it in life to refuse an opportunity that sounds enticing?

AC: After my first film, a producer offered me a film to direct and narrated the story. I did not like it and I told him I needed some time to mull over the proposal. He offered me a cheque payment then and there. I refused to accept the advance, which wasn't an easy decision because I needed the money; at that point, I had never seen that kind of money. He continued to pursue me with money and soon landed up at my house with a demand draft. I had to tell him his story did not excite me. He was relentless and left it with me. I used it as a bookmark for the book I was reading then. After six months, his accountant called me to ask why I had not deposited the demand draft yet. I sent it back to them. I could have said yes and made quick money easily, but I know I would not have been able to sleep thereafter working on a story that had not appealed to me.

How did your writing career take off?

AC: After we finished *Makdee*, Vishal-ji asked me what I was going to do after it. I told him I was making a documentary on mental illness. We were on a train to Goa for some work when he handed me a script and asked me to read it. It was the script of *Maqbool* (2003). At that time, only the first half had been written.

I read it and was blown away. I decided I didn't have a choice, I had to work in a brilliant film like this. It was dark and initially no one was interested in producing it. Finally, it was Bobby Bedi who read the script and agreed to produce it.

I worked on *Maqbool* as an associate director. I was also involved in shot breakdown and shot taking. I used to do that very closely with Vishal-ji. There were a few killing scenes that he asked me to design and write, and a few others that I helped him with. After *Maqbool* he asked me to write the screenplay of *Omkara*.

What was your best experience while working on Omkara?

AC: On *Omkara* I once again worked as an associate director; however, I was not running the set. I was assisting Vishal-ji in the creative aspects of the shoot. In his earlier films, I had ran the set like a first assistant usually does.

While working on *Omkara*, I realized that direction is a completely different beast. You can never know enough about it until you end up doing it yourself. Every time I direct a film, I feel like it is nothing like the ones I've worked on before. Every film, then, is like your first film. Every time, the challenges and experiences are new.

After *Omkara*, Vishal asked me to write the screenplay of his next film, *Kaminey*. And while it was being shot, I did not assist Vishal on it. Instead, I began writing the script of my own first feature as director, *Ishqiya*. By then I was confident and ready to direct.

Three people, including your producer, share the writing credits in your first film . . .

AC: A month or so after *Omkara* finished, I narrated the story of *Ishqiya* to Vishal. He liked it and came on board as a co-writer and was willing to produce it too. We developed it further, but we felt it still needed a lot of improvement; however, we were unable to crack it. He recommended that we get Sabrina Dhawan on board, the writer of *Monsoon Wedding* (2001), and we did. I went to New York to work on the screenplay with Sabrina, and within three months we had a draft ready that Viṣhal approved. That's when I got the green light from Vishal and Shemaroo.

Just like you got stuck while writing, did you get stuck while shooting and didn't know how to proceed and were upfront with your crew?

AC: It happens sometimes, like, during *Udta Punjab*, when we were shooting a stage performance of Tommy Singh, after his release from jail, in a village in Punjab. We needed a crowd of about 800–1000 people but couldn't manage more than 200. We were shooting in a tiny village and the villagers assumed that something suspicious was going on. Yes, the subject of the movie was drugs but we were not on drugs! Some people who had arrived as part of the crowd were looking to do some *panga*, create a scene and disrupt the work, I think, for reasons known best to them. They began to create a ruckus and some people began shouting, 'Hindustan Murdabad, Khalistan Zindabad.' Our talent and crew naturally got scared. If things went out of hand, even the small group of police escorts we had arranged to help with crowd control would have been of no use. I did not know what to do—continue shooting or pack up!

I asked my key crew for help to solve the chaos without disrupting the shoot. Honey Trehan, who had done the casting, the camera crew, all pitched in. They dressed up like the villagers and melted into the crowd discreetly, and started giving instructions in Punjabi to control the crowd. And it worked! The few people who were causing trouble sobered down. We managed to complete the shoot without any untoward incident and within the timeframe we had set for ourselves. Being upfront with your crew helps, as it builds trust and creates a stronger bond with your close collaborators.

You mentioned that self-doubt walks alongside us. Has self-doubt ever overwhelmed you during a shoot?

AC: Self-doubt has put me in a limbo for a long time; however, I have never let it overwhelm me completely. When I started shooting *Ishqiya*, I was confident. I had done the script readings and everything. I was only a bit nervous. We shot the introduction of Naseer and Arshad on the fourth or fifth day of our first shooting schedule. I was very keen to see the rushes because that moment in the script was very special for me. The film opened with their scene. The way we had written it was bizarre! It was the first scene that I had written while scripting in 2006 and it was the first scene we shot during production in 2008. So, I had been waiting for that scene for two years to unfold as a moving image.

When I saw that scene during the edit—we had set up an edit suite in the hotel where we were staying—it looked like shit. I panicked and thought to myself, '*Apni aukaad pata chali?*' I broke my phone in anger. I had an important shoot in the morning and I thought I wouldn't be able to wake up and go on the set. However, I managed to reach on time and smoked a lot of cigarettes because I was shaken up. It was an intimate scene between Vidya and Naseer. I was feeling very low when we started shooting the scene. But the actors performed so well that it came alive and lifted my low spirits. I felt things would work out well. Then the rest of the day I did not think of how badly I had felt I had shot the introduction scene.

Do you have a first-day speech for your crew?

AC: Not really; however, I do make it a point to tell them that on the first schedule they will be highly energized and enthusiastic as they meet the people they are working with and settle into the film-making process. However, what is important to remember is that the real challenge will begin after the first twenty-five days. By then, invariably, fatigue or familiarity will set in. That's when they need to remind themselves that the twenty-sixth or the sixtieth day of the shoot is just as important as the first day.

Let's talk about another significant relationship on set, the director–cinematographer. And why do you think many directors feel it's their most important on-set relationship?

AC: When a director is shooting their film, the most important thing they are doing is capturing the performance in images, for which they have to work closely with the cinematographer. I think the two most people important people on set for a director are the cinematographer and the actor.

Mohana Krishna was the cinematographer for *Ishqiya*, Setu [Satyajit Pandey] for *Dedh Ishqiya* and Rajiv Ravi for *Udta Punjab*. I have wanted to repeat my cinematographer on every film after working with them, but only due to circumstances I could not.

I had actually wanted Tassaduq Hussain for my first film and he was on board. I had worked with him in *Omkara* (2006) and we had become friends. I wanted to work with someone I knew well but our dates did not match. Luckily, I found Mohana just about twenty days before our first schedule. Interestingly, it was his first film too so we were like two fools discovering film-making on the sets together! But it was a good experience working with him. The only brief I gave him was, 'Just take care of the lights and we will discuss shots mutually and do what is necessary.' He told me, 'I will give you whatever you want.' And he did.

I think, the best thing any cinematographer can bring on the table for a director is empowerment. Especially when you are making your first film. A good cinematographer can empower you with the decision as to what works for your script and then find ways to give it to you in the best possible manner. Mohana empowered me as a director. He thrust a lot of responsibility on me and in turn I thrust an equal or more on him and he delivered. He is also an excellent operator. So he could shoot sensitive moves easily. He did all of that very well.

The actor–director relationship is very vocal because they need to communicate effectively on the performance. When an actor is on set, everyone is waiting for them to make some magic and bring the script alive. So, actors are the focus of attention on set. Same for the cinematographer–director—their language is more discreet and often a look shared between the two conveys more than words can. Most often, the cinematographer is the only person who will support you when nobody else does. Invariably, it is the cinematographer who is going to empathize with you when things go wrong on set and offer you some ideas on how to proceed.

Some first-time film-makers feel anxious about where to place the camera. How have you felt about it when you made your first film?

AC: I have never been on the set of my films not knowing where the camera should be. I have to see things clearly before I stage the scene. If not for anything else, but for the sake of clarity of a crew of nearly 250 people. That is the least they can expect from a director.

There is something very interesting that I learnt after becoming a director. I figured out exactly where to place the camera. I know before we stage a scene exactly how the actors need to move in the physical space. Having said that, sometimes I stage a scene exactly the way I had envisioned it but then feel it looks like shit! This has happened with me at least once or twice during every film. Then you have to become a child and seek help. I have confessed to my cinematographer and/or actors that what I had envisioned is not looking good, so maybe we can we try to approach it in some other way. It's very important to be honest and upfront when you feel that things are not working out. It helps in building trust with your cast and crew. People appreciate humility. Then you rework the staging with your actors and cinematographer and, believe me, something wonderful always comes out of it. Most often, when you rework things, your scene becomes ten times better than what you had originally visualized.

You have worked with a large ensemble of actors in Udta Punjab. *Share with us some ways to direct actors.*

AC: Each one of us is unique and so are actors. So, there can never be a one particular way of working with actors. You really have to understand your actor—whether they are stars or a not. Flexibility and adaptability, I think, are two crucial skills that a good director possesses.

Actors will always have different approaches towards their craft. For example, Vidya Balan was keen to do workshops for her role in *Ishqiya*. But Arshad believed he should not, because he has always done his best impromptu, without workshops and intensive readings. I could not convince even Naseer-ji to do workshops; he himself conducts acting workshops! All three main leads of my first film had different approaches towards performance. So, I was getting very antsy before we began shooting *Ishqiya*. Eventually, I literally locked them in a room and told them how I see them as their characters and how I want them to play the nuances, and even confessed my biggest fears about the material. Being candid builds trust.

Sometimes, very good actors become kind of 'comfortable' with the character they are playing, after years of perfecting their craft; this could trap them in a kind of comfort zone. During *Dedh Ishqiya*, Madhuri-ji was doing a great job as Begum Para, but I felt she had perhaps settled in the comfort zone of that character. I needed her to play her bipolar avatar [the character she played in the film, Begum Para, was bipolar] and I needed her to be really edgy in the scene we were shooting. So I lied to Madhuri-ji that the scene was not working and that we needed to reshoot some portions. Can you imagine saying that to such an amazing and experienced actor as her? I immediately sensed that she became a bit uncomfortable or maybe insecure about her ability, or she may have thought that I had no clue about what I was doing. And I got out of her what I needed—the subtext, her anxiety—in the next take. Sometimes a director has to/can lie or trick his or her actor to achieve something like this.

You assisted Vishal Bhardwaj in two children's films, Makdee *and* The Blue Umbrella. *What was your experience working with child actors?*

AC: Normally it's not proper to enact scenes to show your actors [adults] what you want them to do. However, sometimes you need to do exactly that with kids. They imitate very well. They are very pure. Unadulterated with images. If you tell them to do something, and even show it to them, they will do it right away without any inhibition or questions. And, I think, this is easier when you are working on light-hearted moments with kids. I had acted in theatre plays, during my college years, so that experience helped too while working with actors.

What did the brief experience of being a theatre actor give you in the long run?

AC: I had joined an eminent theatre group, Act One, during my third year in college because I enjoyed acting. The experience brought me closer to the stage. It built that impetus in me to be proactive, which forced me to go out and start working.

Theatre is very different from film. And I was not a very good actor, to be honest, but the experience was good. It made me realize how vulnerable actors can be. And, I think, somewhere that experience and knowledge count when you become a director. I am more empathetic towards actors. I understand their problems. You need to make them feel secure; you need to make them feel that you really care for them.

Tell us about staging a scene with actors.

AC: Staging a scene is completely a director's game. [Staging is the organic process of selecting, designing, adapting to, or modifying the performance of actors and/or their space of performance while shooting a shot/scene.] Although you work with actors and even with your cinematographer to an extent, staging a scene is completely dependent on your visualization of that scene first in your head. And then your ability and skill to convey it aptly to the actors.

Who was the editor of your first film and what do good editors bring to the table for a director?

AC: Namrata Rao was the editor on *Ishqiya*, Sreekar Prasad on *Dedh Ishqiya* and Meghna Manchanda Sen on *Udta Punjab*. I did not have an editor when I began shooting my first film. I had wanted to work with Meghna because I was already familiar with her work, having worked with her on *Kaminey*. But our dates did not match. I had liked *Oye Lucky! Lucky Oye!* (2008), which was edited by Namrata Rao, so I went with her. Vishal-ji, my producer, told me to test her by asking her to cut a few scenes. And she did a fairly competent job for someone who didn't even know the script yet.

Technically too she did a very clean job. A lot of editors might know the emotion, but not the technique or the correct pacing. I thought she was very good in that.

I think the three most important people on any film are the writer, director and editor. Because, these are the three people who have nothing but story to work on. An editor is the rewriter, who works not on paper but on celluloid. The editor is the one person who must be brave enough to tell the director which scenes and shots are not working and explain why. And perhaps delete them or reshoot them as per the director's vision. Namrata Rao pointed out a scene which I, as the writer–director, felt was the best. But she said it was ruining the narrative, the larger story. I resisted, but eventually gave in, and am glad now that we deleted it.

You shoot your films in real locations. I did not notice any sets in your first three films.

AC: Sets do not appeal to me. When I write, I figure out the location that the narrative has to be set in. And adapt the script to the location I have in my head. That's the way I like making films. The right sense of place and time is very important to me from the scripting stage itself. There is not a single set in *Dedh Ishqiya*.

How do you treat sound in your films? And your earliest fondest memory of a sound from your formative years?

AC: In *Udta Punjab*, in the stage scene, when Tommy Singh confesses to the crowd that he is no hero, instead a loser because he is addicted to drugs, my sound designer Kunal Sharma created exactly what I was looking for to tell the story by best using silence, music and crowd cheers intermittently. I was not able to achieve it earlier during the edit and it was driving me crazy. I was at peace only when he did the magic for the scene.

I think sound is very important, especially in achieving seamless storytelling. In fact, a good sound cut will lead you into the next scene seamlessly and it will be unnoticeable, more convincing than a good visual cut. So, I pay extra attention to sound transitions between scenes.

There is a fond memory of a sound from my childhood days that I miss even today. Hot summer afternoons in a small town are quiet. Floors are cooled down by washing them with water, and often we lay on mats in the afternoons. We were not allowed go anywhere at that time of the day. The elders would be asleep, but I would not, as my mind would be racing. The only sounds that would puncture the silence of those afternoons would be the whirring of the ceiling fans and the chirping of the sparrows. The sweet chirpings are embedded in me and I miss them acutely in Mumbai. Another sound that I remember fondly is the voice of a radio presenter reading the news or presenting Hindi songs on Akashvani.

Do you make films to raise questions or give answers?

AC: I think, it's more important to raise questions. Society will arrive at the answers by themselves. I would like my films to evoke thought. Whatever I may think my film is about, viewers will take away something different from them. Someone had told me that in my first two films all the main characters were consumed by love. However, I had thought that they were stories of how people used 'love' to manipulate each other for revenge and/or power or money.

Udta Punjab dealt with rampant drug abuse in parts of Punjab. Some people said it was maligning the state. Which was the feedback from a viewer from Punjab that touched you deeply?

AC: I got a call from a woman in Punjab who had lost her son due to drug abuse. She had felt extremely moved after watching the film. She wanted to thank us for making it, for creating an awareness across the state and possibly the nation too. I don't want to be sentimental right now, but the thing is, when we started writing *Udta Punjab*, we had thought that we were hipsters making cool films. Then we went and researched and spent time in Punjab, and realized we had some very heavy responsibilities. On top of everything, it was a movie with mainstream stars such as Shahid and Kareena! Just because you are going to make a mainstream film, you can't just shy away and shortchange people. Sudip and I decided that even if we had to compromise with a few cinematic elements in order to be honest with the subject we were dealing with, we would do so. People should understand those who have suffered due to drugs. Drug addicts should not feel humiliated. Their experiences could show the path to others.

The character played by Alia in Udta Punjab *survives the tragedy she is facing by looking at a billboard that promises a better time in the future. Which billboard do you wake up to today?*

AC: The billboard today is to earn self-respect through the movies I make. Ten years ago, I just wanted to direct. Now if I want to make a mark before I die, I have to leave a body of work that'll earn me a certain amount of dignity, love and respect in the eyes of people.

Someday you may become a parent or you may need to advise someone who is your family about the path to be taken to become a film-maker. What would it be?

AC: If it's my family, I would say, don't take anything from me. Don't expect me to make introductions for you. Also, do not emulate me as a film-maker. Find your own way, your own style, your own voice and your own language. More importantly, strive to become a good human being.

What learnings have you picked up along the way from some film-makers you admire, or just from life in general?

AC: There is a freshness, an innocence, a fascination you begin with when you embark on your career as a film-maker. It's important to keep that intact as the years roll by. Stay 'young' in that sense. Two-time National Award–winner Kamal Swaroop gave me this advice. This applies to all professions—to not let fatigue and familiarity swamp you down over the years. I hope I can remain young in my approach to anything I do in life.

As a film-maker, I think, one way to remain 'young' is to make a different film every time, so that you can discover a new world with every film that you make. My film *Sonchiriya* [it was released in March 2019] was shot in Chambal and it's a subject I had never dealt with before—the blurred lines between justice and revenge. This was also an action film! So, I was really excited!

The many times I have been humbled on set, realizing how someone else's choice and opinion made the scene work better than what I had thought of while writing the script, has taught me that a film-maker is not God. They are not the 'creator'. A director is just a witness to the process of their film's creation, which is created in a collaboration.

Things are going to get much harder, before they become easier. To survive that, you need to keep your heart, mind and soul where they belong. Rooted together, they make a great anchor for our ship to sustain the storms that life invariably brings upon us all.

PERSPECTIVE FROM ANOTHER LENS

Casting Director Honey Trehan speaks of Abhishek Chaubey

My earliest memory of being fascinated by cinema was when I was around five or six years old. My parents had recently bought a TV and the moving and talking images captivated me. I believed the people on screen must be entering our TV from behind. Since then, nothing but the film world enchanted me endlessly.

Abhishek and I have been associated since *Makdee* (2002). I have cast for about forty films, for directors such as Majid Majidi, Ritesh Batra, Gautam Ghosh, Dibakar Banerjee, all films of my mentor Vishal-ji and those of Abhishek's, including the ones in which he worked as an assistant/associate director or writer/director. I was an assistant director and Abhishek was the associate director when I first cast actors in a film. Interestingly, though I was an assistant director, and it was my first film as an assistant, it was I who 'interviewed' Abhishek for a job where he would be my immediate 'boss'.

All the directors I've worked with are great. However, the one great thing about Abhishek is that he maintains a balance between skill and creativity and logistics and administration. As a casting director, I naturally believe that the actors we cast, in association with the director, will deliver the goods. However, sometimes, the actor's performance far exceeds my own expectations or understanding of them. One such casting was that of popular Punjabi actor Diljit Dosanjh as Inspector Sartaj Singh in *Udta Punjab*. Kudos to Abhishek for extracting a far better performance from him and Alia Bhatt.

I do not slot people into roles when I meet them. Rather, I usually cast actors I have met when my instinct shouts out their name to me for a character while I am reading a script.

Abhishek is 100 per cent focused when he works, a no-nonsense person. At the same time he is never averse to anyone's advice. If anyone offers him a suggestion/opinion/advice, he will first assimilate it honestly in his mind and only then react. For me, that makes us [his crew] feel that he values and respects his assistants, technicians and talent—the collaborators on any film. His usual reaction to something that he doesn't feel suits the script is, 'What you are saying is true, from the space you are coming from; however, the effect of that thought on the script will be [. . .] which will not go with the picture we have in mind for this script.' So, even while negating a suggestion he will try and give a reason that justifies why your input does not go with his vision. In a way, he places so much faith in you that you do not want to give him or the film anything less than your 101 per cent!

Abhishek has often given me the responsibility of being the second unit director on his films, and the shots I took have been retained in the final film, such is the faith he has reposed in someone like me who is yet to direct his own first feature. To his credit, he makes me feel I am not just his casting director, now co-producer, and second unit director at times, but also his third hand. He makes everyone on board feel it's their own film and not just his.

Being a writer–director is another great quality in Abhishek; so, he 'lives' the characters we have to cast. Any good casting director will be able to deliver much better if they have a writer as their film's director. Writer–directors, in my little experience, have immense clarity of thought. They have a good understanding of not only the characters, but also the emotional graph of the narrative. That truly is their biggest strength as a director. What Abhishek was able to accomplish with Alia Bhatt as a rural girl from Bihar, in *Udta Punjab*, is a result of his understanding of the character right from its inception.

To conclude, I repeat, Abhishek makes everyone feel they are working on a film along with him. He helps everyone see his vision through their own uniqueness. He gives them ownership of what they are doing on the film. In a way, Abhishek *apne khwaab, humari* [apne crew ki] *aankhon mein bo deta hai* [he can sow the seeds of his dream in our mind too].

KABIR KHAN

*'I think I became a film-maker because of my love for photography
and images, and stories tend to come my way. I script the ones
that stay. Then someone comes along, someone who is willing to
back it financially, and that's how I get to be a film-maker again
and again. Film-making is not a "strategy" for me.'*

FILMOGRAPHY

Kabul Express (2006); *New York* (2009); *Ek Tha Tiger* (2012);
Bajrangi Bhaijaan (2015); *Phantom* (2015); *Tubelight* (2017)

SNEAK PEEK

Kabir was brought up in New Delhi. He claims that photography
was his first love; he was ten years old when his father gifted him
his first camera. He studied economics from Delhi University and
went on to complete a course in photography and films from Jamia
Millia Islamia University's A.J. Kidwai Mass Communication
Research Centre. His first professional job in film-making was
shooting a documentary in Central Asia with Saeed Naqvi in
1992; he wrote about his travels in Central Asia in *Economic Times*
and contributed his travel photographs to various publications.
His first job as a cameraman was on a documentary film shot in
Kashmir for producer Romesh Sharma in 1992. His first feature
film as a cinematographer was with director Gautam Ghosh

in 1994. He directed his first documentary, *The Forgotten Army*, in 1996; he made around sixty documentaries before directing his feature film, *Kabul Express*, in 2006.

Since his first work experience with Saeed Naqvi in 1992 to his first feature film as a director, it had been a journey of nearly twenty-four years.

MY TAKE

The moment I stepped into Kabir's house for the interview, I immediately felt at home. First, it was his domestic help, who ushered me in as if I were a regular visitor, and second, it was his mother who walked into the living room as I was waiting for Kabir and gave me a warm smile.

During the interview, Mini Mathur Khan, a film professional and Kabir's wife, served us two steaming cups of coffee, the foams of which had a beautiful abstract design, and two tiny and cute cookies.

In a memorable moment, their daughter, aged six or seven, crept up to the centre table, unnoticed by us, and stood gazing at the cookies spellbound. Kabir was on a phone call so I asked her if she wanted to have any, but she surprised me by saying, 'No, I only want to touch one of them.'

I lifted the glass cover, convinced that she wanted to eat and not only touch, but she silently and gently poked one of the cookies with her tiny fingers and smiled. She was simply curious! It was so like her film-maker dad—Kabir was always seeking that which went unsaid and unnoticed by most, he hungered after the metatextual elements in life's happenstance, determined to listen to the silence that lies in wait of a conversation.

He is a hands-on, pragmatic and helpful person, I completed the last two hours of the interview driving him around in his car, while he visited locations for his upcoming shoot. In a week, he would be travelling to Beirut for the first principal photography schedule of his next film. Amazingly, he didn't feel stressed out or anxious about his tight schedule.

I remember a dialogue from *Tubelight*: '*Yakeen ki taqat dil mein hoti hai.*' (The strength of one's conviction lies in the heart.) It reaffirmed that I must keep my hopes alive in my heart for many things for as long as it takes. Thank you, Kabir.

THE CONVERSATION

Rakesh Bakshi: *Thank you for being a part of our book. Where did you reside during your formative years? And what was your cultural background?*

Kabir Khan (KK): Pandara Park, Delhi. Our neighbourhood had people from all over the country. It was very enriching, growing up in the midst of a variety of diverse cultures. We celebrated all the festivals together. I did not care much for my religious background until one of my classmates in Class V or VI, I cannot remember when exactly, at Modern School asked me if I were a Hindu or a Muslim. I couldn't answer him so I went home and asked my father. He said, 'Whoever asks you this question again, tell them you are a human being.'

Did you read a lot during your formative years and later?

KK: I was surrounded by books! In fact, even now, while planning the layout of a house, the first thing I do is make space for my books. They have always given us warmth. In fact, they can light up any home. In our Pandara Park house, there used to be a storeroom, where my father kept old magazines. They would be stacked from the floor to the ceiling. I used to be thrilled to pull out a magazine randomly from these towering stacks and read them.

I have many favourite films but no favourite film-maker and it is the same with books. I will read anything that interests me. Peoples Publishing House published great books on world history. I read them all.

Peter Hopkirk had travelled widely where his books are set—Russia, Central Asia, China, India, Pakistan, Iran and Eastern Turkey—and I basked in the glory of all these places. Hopkirk's books spoke a lot about early travellers and how they tried to venture into places that weren't accessible. This invoked a passion for travelling in me. International studies was my father's field in academics, for which he had to travel extensively. I would tell him, 'Baba, I wish I'd get to travel as much as you.' He would return from his trips with pictures and stories. His experiences in Cuba fascinated me and is part of the reason I chose Cuba to shoot *Ek Tha Tiger*.

Do you think reading helps develop writing skills?

KK: Reading expands your horizon. It offers deep insight into other people's thoughts and helps you visualize things much better. I wrote articles for my school and college magazines, and later on contributed to travel features. When I started travelling extensively for work, I wrote features for *Economic Times*. I contributed photographs from my travels to various travel-related publications. All this helped me visualize and write my own features.

Which extracurricular activities may have influenced you creatively towards photography and writing?

KK: I used to draw and sketch a lot as a child, and was fascinated by aeroplanes. I wasn't an active part of the theatre circuit, but I remember playing a role in a production of *West Side Story* (1961) just for fun. I didn't have a specific passion till I turned ten and my dad gave me his camera, a Kodak Retinette. Even then I didn't really want to be a cameraman or a film-maker. But I did know one thing, I too wanted give my son a camera when he turned ten.

My mother, a film buff, would bundle off my sister and me into our Fiat and drive us to Vigyan Bhavan to watch films.

I remember watching *Breathless* (1960) by Jean-Luc Godard there. Over time, we developed a taste for foreign-language films, along with regular Hindi mainstream films that we watched in local cinema halls.

I was also influenced by a close family friend who was a director, Shyam Benegal. My mother had acted in plays directed by him when she used to stay in Hyderabad. I remember watching his first feature film, *Ankur* (1974), and thinking how amazing it was. I also used to watch the first day first show of any of Amitabh Bachchan's films. Our dinner-table discussions often revolved around the art films we saw. It made me realize that my family saw mainstream media as something to be enjoyed and artistic media as something that was meant to inspire you to think.

Your earliest memories of wondering how movies are made?

KK: My earliest memory of a movie is *Bobby* (1973). When I would be watching movies as a child, I would completely believe the 'illusion'. *Star Wars: A New Hope* (1977) was the movie that first made me wonder how these illusions were made. I was old enough to know that the movie hadn't been shot in space! That was when I started reading about movies, trying to answer the many questions I had.

When did you first find out what the term 'director' means?

KK: While watching Benegal's *Ankur*, I realized that for the first time, we were watching a movie in which I was not familiar with the actors. Until then, I had watched films only because of the actors in them. On the way back, my parents started discussing the director of the film and how he had made it. I asked my mother what a 'director' meant and she explained their role. Thereafter, I began understanding the process—somebody writes a story, actors are cast and it is the director who tells the actors and everybody else what to do.

Did you get attracted to film-making thereafter?

KK: I was a floater and I am floating even today! I think, I became a film-maker because of my love for photography and images, and stories tend to come my way. I script the ones that stay. Then someone comes along, someone who is willing to back it financially, and that's simply how I get to be a film-maker again and again. Filmmaking is not a 'strategy' for me.

I was keen on studying law. However, I had started taking pictures since my teens. I never thought of films as a career until I joined Jamia after my graduation. After I graduated in economics, I did not know what to do. My sister, a year older to me, on the other hand, was very clear that she was going to learn film-making. She was planning to apply for Jamia's mass communication course. She often spoke about the university and I felt it was a cool place to learn photography and film. I told her, '[. . .] whatever application form you are getting for MCRC Jamia, get one for me too.'

I enjoyed the process of application. We had to watch some films and analyse them. Both of us got through! Honestly, I wasn't dying to get into Jamia, but when I did, I thought, 'Okay! Let's go with it.' I instinctively felt that that was where I belonged. The moment they gave me a Nikon FM2 camera at Jamia and told me, 'Here's free film; here's whatever lenses you want; go out and take photographs [. . .] go shoot!', I said to myself, 'This is exactly what I've always wanted to do! This is what I do on holidays anyway.' Still photography was my entry point into the visual medium. I was first enchanted by the craft of taking still images, telling stories through static.

I think, I started developing a sense of aesthetics since childhood, which became structured through professional education in early adulthood. When you begin reading and studying about aesthetics, trying to consciously do things that you've been taught, it becomes even more deeply internalized. It becomes intuitive.

Rajeev Lochan, an artist, who was director of National Gandhi Museum of Art (NGMA), taught us visual arts. He made us do strange exercises to develop our sense of composition. I haven't done anything as interesting since then. His methods really made me arrive at my own definition and sense of aesthetics, my own sense of composition. He used to keep telling me, 'After this course, if you don't do a course in fine arts, you'll regret it for the rest of your life.' I never got down to pursuing fine arts, because immediately after Jamia, I started working as a professional cameraman. However, that was a blessing too, because that's when I met Saeed Naqvi, the film-maker who soon became a mentor. Saeed Saab would travel around the world, shooting documentaries and I would eagerly accompany him.

How did you get your first break as a cameraman? What were the memorable experiences while shooting documentaries?

KK: When I graduated from Jamia, I decided, since I was new to film-making, I should begin as a freelance cameraperson. Moreover, it paid very well. My first stint was with Saeed Saab in 1992.

Director Romesh [Ramesh] Sharma, of *New Delhi Times* (1986), was the external examiner for our final degree film at Jamia. He told me he liked my work and added, '[. . .] after your graduation, get in touch with me.' I met Romesh again sometime in 1992. He told me he was starting a project for Doordarshan and wanted me to accompany him to Bombay [Mumbai] for a ten-day shoot. I agreed immediately!

After Romesh saw the footage I had shot in Mumbai, he was impressed enough to offer me another job, which was a turning point in my career as a cameraman. We were shooting every day for a year in various locations. I learnt how to frame, how to recognize light and the light source. When I began directing films, I was able to prepare my shot-breakdown within five minutes of reaching the location, with my director of photography.

When I reach any set or location, I instinctively know where the camera should be placed, which angle we should begin with and which lens to be used.

Did you ever face any extraordinary situations while shooting documentaries across the world that helped you grow professionally?

KK: Yes. It was 1994 and Romesh asked me to shoot a documentary in Kashmir. This was at a time when there was a lot of conflict in Kashmir. I had gone trekking in Kashmir as a student and during that time, made some friends there. I sought their help to get in touch with the Hizbul Mujahideen. Before we met with members of the group, we came across two men who were suspicious of our intentions and threatened to kill us. Eventually, the local journalist who was guiding us had to come to our rescue and assure the men that we did not wish to stir trouble.

However, once, as we were emerging from our houseboat on Dal Lake in Srinagar, two boats silently approached us. There were armed militants on board who demanded to know what we were doing there. They interrogated us for nearly forty-five minutes and went through all our tapes and recordings. We told them that we were there to interview both the Border Security Force (BSF) and Hizbul Mujahideen, and that the former were aware of our plans. We had kept both sides informed of our sincere intentions from day one. That helped us earn a certain degree of trust. Such experiences change your perception of life.

We faced dangerous situations in Afghanistan too, when we first went there to shoot a documentary and later, *Kabul Express*. I believe, you may lead a more comfortable and safe life shooting in a city like Delhi, and getting well paid for it too, but you need to push the envelope and explore new territories for new experiences, the prospect of which has always excited me.

I once took a dangerous decision to shoot a documentary in Afghanistan, on which my first feature *Kabul Express* was based. When we got the news that the Taliban was collapsing, we—Romesh and I—decided to make a documentary on Afghanistan. The first scene in that film, when John and Arshad jump off the helicopter, is exactly how Romesh and I arrived in Afghanistan in 2001.

How did you land your first job as a cinematographer?

KK: Romesh introduced me to his friend, Gautam Ghosh, a film-maker. Gautam was also a cinematographer and we were both young and trying to do crazy things. He was enthusiastic about my work and told me he was making a once-in-a-lifetime-kind-of project—a documentary on the Silk Route! I told him my very first project after college was with Saeed Naqvi in Central Asia. Gautam realized I had already travelled and shot extensively in the places he intended to shoot. I also informed him of some of the problems we had faced while shooting there. Eventually, I admitted that I would give my right arm to shoot a film on the Silk Route. He didn't take my arm but he hired me. Experience has always helped me land a project and even helped me write my first feature. It all matters. It always does. And, of course, before we left, I read extensively on the Silk Route. I hated being in a place and not knowing too much about it.

Kabul Express was inspired by your own documentary on Afghanistan. Tell us how it came about and your experiences there.

KK: Romesh was in a collaboration with an American company, Tele Productions International, that wanted us to make a documentary. I suggested we go to Afghanistan and do a feature on what was happening there post the disastrous five-year Taliban rule. He asked me who in their right mind would agree to visit Afghanistan during such a time. I said I would.

Tele Productions agreed to our proposal, because until then, the Americans visiting Afghanistan were largely journalists who were only reporting hard news; nobody had tried to shoot a documentary feature. Tele Productions told us not to worry about the budget and do what we needed to make the documentary. We were determined because we knew such an opportunity, in such times, would perhaps not arrive again.

How did your work on documentaries, before Kabul Express, *help you as a director?*

KK: Before I wrote *Kabul Express*, I'd already made around sixty documentaries. The twelve years that I worked on documentaries really helped me professionally. Those years shaped me to be the person and director I am today—the way I approach stories, the way I carry out my research, the places I travel to, the characters I write.

Documentary film-making has been one of my greatest assets as a director. I think, just the sheer speed and raw intuition with which I can look at a location, a situation, a circumstance and react to them is thanks to my years of shooting documentaries. You don't get stressed because it's not going the way you had meticulously planned. You subconsciously learn to react to any eventuality. You don't get thrown off by sudden changes in situations, even if they threaten your schedule. They teach you to embrace the reality behind *and* in front of the camera.

My experience with documentaries is also why, in my films you will see an absence of sets for the most part. I hate shooting on sets because it begins to take control of my creative energy, overwhelm my freedom to adapt and change something. I feel restricted on sets. I don't feel excited. I don't feel like I'm playing with all the elements that can arrive with the breeze through an open window. I feel like I'm missing the thing that would give me something beyond what I wrote and thought. A lot of film-makers love working on sets and would rather set up everything inside a controlled environment. I don't. I would rather take my chances with the sun and the rain and the wind. I would rather embrace the dynamics of befriending the unknown.

If you can change and adapt to the way things are happening, unfolding, unravelling naturally, I think that adds momentously to the whole texture of the film, making it richer, more gorgeous and more meaningful.

What made you script Kabul Express *as your first feature film?*

KK: After the 9/11 terror attack in New York, I found myself doing a lot of documentary work in and about Afghanistan. Eventually, I shot two or three documentaries in Afghanistan, as guerrilla short films. I had a huge number of real stories and anecdotes from my personal experiences in Afghanistan, which would churn in my conscious and subconscious mind, and I realized what I had experienced in Afghanistan would make a great story by itself. Thus inspired, I sat down one day to write the story of *Kabul Express*.

In hindsight, it was easy to put it all down as a screenplay, because I basically just had to string together our experiences. I wrote the script within two or three months, which, I think, has been the fastest that I've written a script to date.

Considering your films may reflect socio-political themes, do you make them to raise questions or answers?

KK: Neither. Primarily, I just want to tell a story. But I do like to tell a story against a certain socio-political context, which has some sort of resonance, first within me, and then, in society. Having said that, my storytelling is neither agenda-driven nor thought-driven. But, yes, I think, I would like to say that I make films that raise some questions and may sometimes give a few answers that have not been heard before.

How did you get someone to produce Kabul Express?

KK: I was married by then and Mini was a VJ with MTV. So, she had a bit of an 'engagement' with Bollywood people; MTV VJs were celebrities back then. Mini knew some well-placed people and got me some important numbers of people I could pitch my script to. Jaideep Sahni, a screenplay writer who had written *Khosla Ka Ghosla* (2006), was a friend, and helped me procure the numbers of actors and producers. I started contacting them.

However, whoever I narrated the story of *Kabul Express* to reacted with, 'Wow! What a lovely story! But it is a very "different" film! Difficult to make.' They felt there was no market for such a film. I was clear that I would be able to shoot it in Kabul, because for me, Kabul was not a location, it was a character in my film; and I had already shot two documentaries there and survived. I was confident that I'd be able to pull off a feature film there.

Meanwhile, I never gave up on trying to cast well-known actors. I went to all kinds of producers and production houses—new, old, semi-old, semi-new, small, very small, medium, big, very big. But I never approached Yashraj Films, because conventional wisdom told me, 'Yashraj? To produce this kind of film? No way! Are you crazy!'

While I waited for producers to revert, I began to look for actors myself. I approached Arshad Warsi. Arshad's wife is my wife's friend so it wasn't that difficult to meet him. He read the script and was immediately on board. Then, I met John Abraham and he too agreed to be in the film. With these two in, I thought my chances of getting a producer would increase exponentially. However, I was proved wrong. I still could not convince anyone to make the film.

An executive producer friend of mine, without my knowledge, had given the script to Adi [Aditya Chopra of Yashraj Films], because, at that point, he was looking for films outside his comfort zone. This friend knew about it because he was working with Adi. I received a call out of the blue from Yashraj Films. The caller informed me that Aditya Chopra wanted to meet me. I thought it was a prank. I said, 'Yeah, yeah, sure. Like, hell! Adi Chopra would want to meet me, a first-time film-maker whose script is nowhere close to the kind of films Yashraj makes!' However,

I eventually realized the caller was serious and was indeed calling me from Yashraj Films!

Within five minutes of that call, Jaideep Sahni called me. He had read my script long ago, because I had bounced it off him as a friend. He said Adi wanted to meet me because he had read my script and liked it. Later, I found out that when Adi had mentioned my script to Jaideep, he had replied that he already knew about it because he had read it long ago and liked it too, and had even suggested changes. Adi had then asked him about me and Jaideep had told him, 'Kabir's a friend and he is capable of directing this film.' And that's when Adi decided to meet me and his office called me.

It was a momentous feeling when I entered Yashraj Films' office to meet this mythical character, producer and director called Aditya Chopra. When I met him, he said, 'I have read your script, it really moved me and I want to produce it. When can we start?' And that was it! Adi stood by me like a rock, from day one.

You faced a lot of 'no-s' before getting that one yes from producers. How important is it to say no, now that you are successful?

KK: You must have a long-term goal if you want to resist the temptation to say yes to something that sounds good but is not meant for you. While I was working as a cinematographer in Delhi, I was being paid quite handsomely to shoot documentaries. But I knew deep down that if I didn't move to Bombay, my ambition to be a film-maker wouldn't be fulfilled. I could have either continued and maybe become the king of cinematography in Delhi, keep shooting documentaries and making good money, or I could have foregone that life for the insecurity of making a fresh start in Mumbai. If you have that long-term goal, you have to pursue it, relentlessly, whatever be the cost.

After the box-office success of *Ek Tha Tiger*, I received many proposals, some from stars, some from star producers and corporates, who offered astronomical fees to direct a film with them. I refused only because their scripts did not excite me. I didn't join this industry to make money. I joined this industry because I wanted to become a film-maker and tell stories.

Considering you had never worked with actors before as you shot real people all your professional life until then, did you conduct actors' workshops for Kabul Express?

KK: Not much. *Kabul Express* was literally guerrilla film-making! Particularly because it was shot in Kabul, which was engulfed in sporadic firing and bombing even while we were shooting there. Despite losing formal control of Afghanistan in 2001, some pockets of Taliban continued to fight against NATO's International Security Assistance Force (ISAF), from 2002 onwards, in a bid to recapture land and influence. As a film unit shooting during that period, we were literally jumping in and out of real locations, doing stuff quickly and moving on to the next location. I would narrate the lines from the script on location and ask my actors how they would say them. On hearing the lines from them, I would quickly consent to their dialogue or suggest a few changes and immediately shoot the scene. So, I could not attempt any kind of a structured script rehearsal or extensive reading.

Having said that, we did go through the lines with our actors in Mumbai before we left for Kabul. My aim was to make them aware of the geopolitical situation in Afghanistan—where they would be, what was it that they were seeking to uncover, the context of the resident population there, how they reacted to journalists, what we, the crew, were supposed to do when we landed there amongst them and how to interact with the locals, how we were going to shoot in a city whose political atmosphere was extremely volatile. All this information made my actors understand what their characters meant to the story. And once an actor can see and feel the context of his character's situation, his personal characteristics fall in place naturally.

I believe in line readings only to an extent. If you take an actor through too many script workshops, too many line readings, it just takes away the spontaneity and joy from them, and even me, of discovering things on location. I believe in giving minimal directions to my actors during line readings.

Once an actor understands the context of a film, especially ones that have a social, political or economic context, they can easily locate their character's reaction in that situation. The information I provide helps them in arriving at their character of their own accord; I don't really have to 'direct' them.

Can you tell us how you usually direct an actor?

KK: Like I said, I believe in giving minimal directions on the first take. I just convey the context of the scene to them, tell them about the backdrop of the moment they are in at that point of the screenplay, where it's headed, and that's it. Once I give them that information, I wait to watch what the actor is going to give me in the very first take, or the rehearsal, building on whatever little I have told them. From that a few questions get answered. For example, are they on the same page as me? Have they gone somewhere else? Is the path they've taken more interesting than mine? Should I explore that zone, their intuition, their understanding of my scene? Or have they missed the mark completely? Then and only then do I start putting in or pulling out from their understanding and performance.

Frankly, I don't know whether it's a good thing or a bad thing, the way I function with my actors, and I do not know how others direct. It's worked for me so far, or so I feel.

Is there a specific skill to directing actors?

KK: Yes, it definitely requires a skill. But I think it's more intuitive and not really something that can be explained or taught. But it can be honed, just like any other skill. Just like a director arrives with a learned skill set, so does an actor. But at the same time, I think, what's more important is the actor's temperament, their approach to life, to directors. All that determines how you deal with an actor when you are directing them.

Who was the cinematographer of your first film?

KK: Anshuman Mahaley. He was from Jamia too. Honestly, when you are working on your first film, you want to ally with people you're friends with, who would support you, who are on the same page as you. It's not that you're being selective. You create a comfortable space where there is a certain sense of shared aesthetics and sensibilities and you don't tussle much while making choices. And in film-making we make hundreds of friends daily.

   Maybe because I was a cinematographer, I was, at some point, a little anal about how I wanted things to be. It's always good to have somebody who has collaborated with you before, with whom you've shared a past; ego or pride isn't likely to come between you. You will have healthy discussions and reach a consensus more easily.

You are a cinematographer too. How do you collaborate with various cinematographers?

KK: I never get into the nitty-gritty of cinematography techniques. As long as the broad vision and the broad style matches, it's the DOP's prerogative to decide how they're going to put the two together. I won't direct them on their execution of the lighting or the lenses. I only discuss what I need at a broader lever, 'This is the mood I want; this is the kind of feeling I want to evoke [. . .].' Then it's up to the DOP to set up the lighting the way they want. I can suggest that we should go a bit closer if I feel I need more intensity or wider or even a bit higher, but these are minor tweaks.

Do you have a favourite lens?

KK: For cinema the tele is definitely my favourite, because I like the image it produces. I like the boldness. I like the visual quality. It allows me to centre my attention, the audience's attention, to something that I like, something I need emphasized. A tele image has less distraction, it's to the point, it cuts well and it cuts nicely with other shots.

I say this more from the perspective of a budding photographer, because, for the most part, the same aesthetics carry on to films but sometimes certain scenes require a different sort of lensing, in which case I either prefer to go pretty wide or go pretty tele. I am not too fond of the mid-range 50 mm lens.

Having said that, if you ask me, 'Which is the one lens you would carry if you could carry only one?' I'll probably say, 'Give me a 50 mm lens.' It's the one lens that you can, depending on how you use it and your distance from the subject, treat as a wide and a tele.

Who was the editor of Kabul Express? Tell us your views on editing.

KK: Amitabh Shukla, a friend of mine from Delhi University. I think a good editor can challenge your comfort zones and bring an alternative perspective to your material that affects the pace of your storytelling. Directors can tend to be a little indulgent with shots. We've shot it and we remember the effort that's gone into it and can get attached to the footage. There have been times when I've realized that I'm trying to push a shot or a scene even when it's evident that it's not contributing to the narrative.

The pace is very important because at the end of the day, a good screenplay is effective only if the pace is correct. A good screenplay on paper can be destroyed by a bad edit. And when I say bad edit, I mean even one extra second in a scene can sometimes spoil the intended effect. I have watched so many films in which, say, the humour of the scene is negated by that one lingering second or because the camera moved away a second earlier.

Ego management, is that another skill a director needs?

KK: Oh, yes! It's the biggest skill of a director. And I'm not talking exclusively of the cast but the whole crew. Even the way you tell the lensman to bring a lens to you is part of ego management. Each member of the crew is crucial to the production and filming process and you don't want anyone to be pissed off at you.

Direction is actually all about people management. Most of the creative work ends once you finish writing the script. Once you've moved into production, it's all about channelling the creative energies of your seventy or eighty team members towards what you want on the screen. And I repeat, when I say ego, it's not only about superstars. It's about every single person involved in the making of a film.

When we say ego, we often mean pride and ignore the sense of dignity that everybody has. Everybody tries to protect their dignity. While working, a certain professional hierarchy is created that needs to be carefully negotiated. I believe a director must speak with as much dignity to a person on the lowest rung of the ladder as he would to the one on the top. It is essential for the entire team to be fully involved in and give their best to the production process. I think a very important element of the director's work is to make sure that *everybody* in the team is respected, is in good spirits and is working happily.

If your child came up to you and said, 'Dad, I want to be a film-maker,' what would you advise them to do?

KK: 'Go for it!' I won't point them to any path. You have to follow your dreams, you have to pursue what you want. One thing I would say for sure is that your education has to be complete, because I believe education expands your horizons and helps you perceive the world differently. To pursue a career without being educated would be unfair to yourself and to the dream you're chasing.

I would also inculcate a love for travel in them, which, I believe, is the best education. You can read a million books about a country but the second-hand information would pale in comparison with what you can glean by visiting that country. One trip to that country and you would realize what the country, the people and their culture are all about.

I've said it before and I'll say it again, Saeed Saab has been one of the biggest influences in my life, because those five or six years years that I travelled with him to those fifty countries, shaped me and changed me as a person. I was suddenly more confident, more aware, more perceptive to things, more sensitive to situations.

Is there something you would want to tell today's generation from all your experiences so far?

KK: No, yaar. I would feel too pompous to tell anything to anybody. However, there is one thing that I managed to do in my life: follow my passion. When my passion was trekking, I did that. When my passion was to go on long adventurous drives across the world, I did that. So, I would just say follow your passion because there's nothing more rewarding than that and if your passion becomes your profession, you're a very lucky person.

PERSPECTIVE FROM ANOTHER LENS

Cinematographer Aseem Mishra speaks of Kabir Khan

Till now I've shot five films with Kabir as a director of photography. The first feature film I shot was *New York* (2009), then *Ek Tha Tiger, Phantom, Bajrangi Bhaijaan* and *Tubelight*. However, we've known each other since our college days. We graduated from Kirori Mal College, Delhi University. After completing our higher education and graduating from MCRC Jamia, Kabir was shooting documentaries for Saeed Naqvi. When he decided to shift to Mumbai, he recommended me to Saeed Naqvi Saab, as his [Kabir's] replacement as a cameraman. In fact, even before that he had approached me to be his cinematographer for *New York*. In 2004, it was Kabir who suggested that I shift to Mumbai to work as a cinematographer on features.

The relationship between the director of photography and the director is an intense and complex one. There are a lot of benefits if they both know each other well and are in sync. This happens when both of them think along similar lines. You don't have to be a mirror image of each other but it doesn't hurt to share some commonalities. *Tubelight* was my fifth film with Kabir and we are still going strong. We respect each other. We have similar sensibilities when it comes to ethics and aesthetics. We share similar political and social views.

A lot of work goes into framing a shot. You don't simply aim the camera and record. At least, I don't function like that. We tell a story in that frame. That frame is the brainchild of the director and the cinematographer. In fact, when Kabir and I shoot on location, most of our conversation is very cryptic and non-verbal. We don't discuss shots on location in front of the actors. He knows exactly how I frame the shots and is clear about his vision. After years of working with him, I know exactly what kind of magnification and focus he is looking for. That's the kind of comfort you build when you work with the same director time and time again. I would also like to point out that the same director and DOP can also produce very different films altogether. Just look at *New York* and *Bajrangi Bhaijaan*!

Sometime in 2005, Kabir called me to shoot a TV commercial he was directing. We shot around four to five commercials together. After wrapping up, he invited me to his office saying, 'I am directing my next feature and I think you will connect to the story, so come to the office.' That's how our first feature collaboration began.

He described the plot very concisely, saying it was about a sleeper cell that is activated. He told me he wanted the shots to be rough and realistic. I was okay with that. I understood that he was looking for a cinematographer who knew how to light it and shoot it realistically. He must have thought that as we were from the same documentary background, it would be easy for us to communicate on this kind of film.

Because we shared a similar sense of aesthetics, sensibilities and perception, we were in sync nine times out of ten, regardless of whose call it was. This one time we were on location and I suggested shooting from a particular axis where the lighting, due to the position of the earth and the sun, was great. However, to shoot the entire scene in that lighting Kabir would've had to get it done by 2.30 p.m. When I told him this, he was confident we would pull it off and we began shooting immediately. That day, not only did we finish that scene, but we also shot another one with the same lighting, all before 2.30 p.m.

Despite being a cameraman, Kabir never gets into lensing. He knows that space very clearly and respects his cinematographers enough to trust them with the lens. He spends as much time as possible before a take with his actors. He doesn't interfere with the job of the cinematographer after he is hired. He trusts his own decision to hire this person and in their professional abilities.

We both see the value of a twilight shoot, and even understand the pressures on a director and a cinematographer to pull off such a shoot. In *New York*, there is a scene between Irrfan and Neil against the Manhattan cityscape in the background. That day the sky was cloudy and the crew was certain we would not be able to capture the skyline because of the poor light. We had got permission to shoot there with a lot of difficulty and it was valid for only one day.

I studied the position of the sun and the movement of the clouds, and told Kabir, considering the position of the clouds and the sun, the clouds will move in one direction and with the earth's movement, within three hours the sun will appear in that part of . . . We must not pack up as yet.' He agreed. He took a leap of faith and trusted me and it worked brilliantly for him.

I can say that our experience of shooting documentaries, shooting in real locations and knowing how the northern hemisphere reacts in certain weather conditions have made us both instinctive. We take calls like that.

Once, an actor who was working with me for the first time, anxiously asked Kabir, 'I do not see your cinematographer using many lights, which others usually do. Are you sure it is all right? I hope he knows what he is doing!' I think some actors have a preconceived notion about people from a documentary background. They fear they may not be using adequate light to shoot them or that they do not know how to shoot features. Kabir assured the actor that I knew my job well and there was nothing to worry about. Discreetly, he told me to place some 'dummy' lights in the background and switch them on to make it seem like the actor was subjected to brighter lights. I did that, just to make the actor psychologically comfortable. I think Kabir handled that tricky situation very well, talking to both the actor and me sensitively and intelligently without being dishonest to either of us or to our film. The actor had a very good skin tone and facial structure, I did not want to/need to pump light on his face unnecessarily, because that would have created shadows and disturbed the naturally beautiful complexion.

Typically, when we shoot an action scene or an intense scene, Kabir and I discuss it thoroughly. We break down the scene in a way that is comfortable to the actors and convenient for lensing or lighting set-ups. After our discussion, Kabir leaves me to join the actors, knowing the next time we will chat is when we have to break down the next scene.

Kabir is very specific when he is shooting a scene. He doesn't shoot a scene over and over again. He believes that shooting the same dialogues time and time again would cause the actor to get desensitized to the emotion behind the dialogue. He is one of the few directors who—even while shooting in digital, which is far cheaper than film stock—will still shoot cut to cut and not go for the traditional coverage manner of shooting.

Kabir is honest and does not believe in dictating terms to people. He has a robust personality. Even after the shoot, he would want to go for a run or suggest we eat together in some special place he has heard about. If the location is nearby, he will always prefer to walk. Post shoot, he is fun to hang out with. When we were shooting in Cuba, during *Ek Tha Tiger*, he would take us to museums and other places of interest.

Kabir is also very empathetic; if somebody is unwell and can't come in, he handles it rationally and sensitively. He often underplays his own illness, lest it get in the way of work or having fun or seeing new places. Once, we were going to see some place in Cuba and he was feeling ill, I think it was food poisoning, but he absolutely refused to see the doctor.

He is upfront and not afraid to converse or contradict people who may have more experience than him. I have seen him fire a senior American action director who had not done a good job on the shoot. He's a very secure individual, both mentally and intellectually. He isn't pretentious. He knows the more knowledge you have, the better it is for everyone.

Best of all, Kabir is the first one to arrive on the set and the last one to leave.

NANDITA DAS

'While film-making is taught in schools, and one can learn the techniques and skills, it remains an art. Art is inexplicable and spontaneous. There is no set formula for it. It is alchemy. I became a director, by default, with Firaaq, not because I wanted to be a "director", but because I wanted to tell a story that needed to be told. For me, film-making is a means to an end. As a first-time director, I experienced the magic of every phase of film-making. I stumbled, learnt and discovered. The sense of wonderment with every discovery is unforgettable and that experience will always be special for me.'

FILMOGRAPHY

Firaaq (2008); *Manto* (2018)

SNEAK PEEK

Born in Mumbai, Nandita Das spent most of her life in Delhi, and moved back to Mumbai when she was forty. Her father is a painter and her mother, a writer. From a young age, she learnt Odissi, pottery and music. She speaks five languages.

While Nandita acted in *Parinati* (1986) directed by Prakash Jha, it is Deepa Mehta's *Fire* (1996) that is considered her acting debut. Thereafter, she has gone on to star in more than forty feature films in ten different languages. She directed her first feature film, *Firaaq*, in 2008.

MY TAKE

I had a massive crush on Nandita Das ever since I saw her first film. Nearly two decades later, while I was on my way to meet her for this anthology, a powerful image reappeared to me, that of her character Sanwari's, from director Jagmohan Mundhra's *Bawandar* (2000).

Bawandar is based on the true story of Bhanwari Devi, a gang-rape survivor from Rajasthan, who is now a social worker and continues to fight for justice even after twenty-six years. The film showed how rape was used as an instrument by the socially and politically powerful to 'teach a lesson' to a 'low-caste' woman. The trauma, public humiliation, and legal and social injustice that Bhanwari Devi endured overwhelmed me. She fought against the currents of an unhelpful society, close relatives, and a corrupt police force and judicial system. For an actor in her formative years to portray such a character, she needed to have an incredible amount of trust on her director.

I had wondered why a young actor like her would choose such a role. I understood her choice only when I learnt, after meeting her, about her association and background as an actor with Safdar Hashmi's street-theatre group, Jan Natya Manch, a significant voice in Indian socio-political theatre.

When I arrived at her house for this interview, the first things I noticed were a large window in her living room that let in a lot of natural light and a mini library. A few ink paintings adorned the walls of the room. On closer inspection, I realized they were painted by her father, Jatin Das.

I must mention here, from the innumerable films she has worked on as an actor, I have liked her the most in *Parinati*, *Fire*, *Bawandar*, *Earth* (1996) and *Hari-Bhari* (1999).

When she walked into the living room, I realized she was shorter than I had imagined her to be, maybe because the characters she played had a 'large' presence in that film's narrative.

No words can convey aptly the enthusiasm with which she speaks about things she is passionate about, other than film-making, like her family or even inclusiveness. She was so eloquent and expressive that I drifted into the world she was speaking about. I thought, 'Oh God, her interview is going to be a nightmare to edit.' But it truly was a wonderful, one-of-a-kind experience.

When Nandita directed her first theatrical play, *Between the Lines*, in 2012, I was excited to see what a person like her would create—a person who read between the lines and was constantly seeking the subtext, the unsaid, the things people really meant but did not or could not voice. I eagerly went to watch the first show. The play dealt with everyday gender inequality presented through a compelling drama between a husband and wife.

THE CONVERSATION

Rakesh Bakshi: *Thank you for being a part of this anthology. So tell me where you were born and brought up.*

Nandita Das (ND): I was born in Bombay. When I was six months old, my parents moved to Delhi, where I've spent most of my life.

I've heard your parents come from very diverse cultures and they made sure you travelled a lot in your childhood. How has this influenced you?

ND: Like any other child, my upbringing and the exposure my parents gave me impacted me greatly. They took us to their respective family homes every summer holiday. My brother and I would go to Baripada, a small town in Odisha, my father's hometown. We would also visit our maternal grandparents whose house was behind the Metro Theatre in Bombay. My parents spoke many languages, had friends from the world of art and literature, and were deeply secular, egalitarian and inclusive without being burdened by labels. So it was easy for me to instinctively imbibe all of this. I have to say that things you experience first-hand, by living them, have a much stronger impact on you compared to something that is just taught to you. These experiences are always accessible to you, even much later in life. They become part of who you are.

Were you a voracious reader in your early years?

ND: I was. I read a lot of fiction from around the world—Gabriel Garcia Marquez, John Steinbeck, John Berger, Nadine Gordimer, Toni Morrison and Khalil Gibran were some of my favourite authors. I enjoyed reading plays by Anton Chekov and Bertolt Brecht too. I also read some Hindi and Urdu literature [in Devanagari]. These books have helped me understand the human condition and the complexity of relationships and socio-political contexts. They inspired me. The biography of Charlie Chaplin was one of the first and most amazing biographies I read. As my mother is a writer and was the director of the National Book Trust, she took me to many book fairs and got many books home. I distinctly remember the colourful Russian books that had lovely illustrations.

Did your hobbies or pursuits shape your choice to be an actor?

ND: I never had specific career goals or ambition to become an actor or film-maker. Acting was an accident. As a child, I did participate in a lot of plays, elocutions and recitations. I also learnt classical dance and music. But at that time, it was not a step towards a career in acting. It was simply because I loved doing it.

During my summer holidays, both in Baripada and Bombay, my cousins and I would come together and organize what we called a 'variety programme' for our friends and relatives. We would erect a cloth curtain, create a makeshift stage and rehearse for plays, dance and musical performances. In Bombay, we would ticket our shows and whatever money we saved, we would spend on watching a film at Liberty Cinema. It was so much fun!

As a child, I also painted, learnt pottery and enjoyed gardening. Everything we do as children adds to the way we look at life as adults.

Did you participate in theatre during your college years?

ND: Yes, I did. I thoroughly enjoyed travelling and performing at different places with Jan Natya Manch. I remember Safdar Hashmi telling me often, 'You should take up acting more seriously.' I'd always reply, 'Never!' Sadly, he never got to see his prophetic advice become a reality. I still can't believe that he was brutally murdered. I am fortunate to have been touched by his art, his humanity, his passion, his commitment and his life. He sowed the seed of my engagement with art as a means to social change. This is the way I view my creative work and this understanding was aided greatly by him.

In many ways, this was also my first socio-political training. Thereafter, I did my master's in social work and joined NGOs that worked on issues of human rights and social justice. All of these experiences have greatly impacted the choices I have made as an actor and film-maker. This exposure to the realities of life beyond my own deeply touched me. It almost compelled me to want to do something about it.

Your parents had a diverse group of friends, many of whom had art and film backgrounds. Did people from the film industry visit your house? Did they in any way encourage you to join films?

ND: My father knew many people from the film world, such as Shabana Azmi, Amol Palekar, Om Puri, Shyam Benegal, Naseeruddin Shah and Muzaffar Ali. During college, Prakash Jha asked me to act in a film called *Parinati*. The writer of *Parinati*, Vijaydan Detha, knew my mother well. As there was a strike on at college and the script was powerful, I thought it would be an interesting experience. Surekha Sikri, a friend of my parents, was playing the lead and coaxed them. My father finally agreed. It was amazing to shoot in the Rajasthan desert, in the middle of a freezing winter!

When I was around twenty, film-maker Saeed Mirza, also a friend, asked my father if I would act in his film, *Naseem*. My father felt I would be distracted from my postgraduate studies. He also felt that the film industry was all about quick fame and money and that one would easily lose one's path. Deep down, I felt the same. My mother was less sceptical, but I ended up not doing it.

It was later, in 1996, that I worked on *Fire* that led me to other acting projects.

You never saw acting or direction as a career. Yet, you have remained committed to this profession successfully for over two decades.

ND: I have remained as committed to films as I have to my other interests, such as social advocacy and writing. Even today, acting remains an interest and not a profession. It has always been the story and the experience of being on a shoot that have drawn me in. I was always more attracted by the script and the director's vision of translating it into a film than the role, as is usually the case for an actor. There were times when I acted in four films in a year and there were years in which I didn't act at all. Acting has paid my bills but I have never seen it as a career. I have always wanted to be part of different stories that I felt need to be told.

As a director, one gets to tell the story one wants to and not just be a part of it. Both *Firaaq* and *Manto* were not stories I had looked for; they found me. In retrospect, maybe the director in me has always been more present than the actor. I have done many so-called 'ordinary' roles because I really liked the stories. Perhaps, there was always a director in me that I wasn't aware of.

What's your first memory of cinema?

ND: We hardly saw films in our growing up years. My earliest memory of a film is Rajesh Khanna's *Haathi Mere Saathi* (1971). I was introduced to cinema during my college years. Many of my friends wanted to be film-makers and took me to film festivals and embassy screenings. I thoroughly enjoyed the experience of watching independent films from all over the world. At that time, the thought of becoming an actor or a director didn't even cross my mind!

400 Blows (1959) and *Jules et Jim* (1962), both directed by François Truffaut, and *Wild Strawberries* by Ingmar Bergman are some of my first memories of watching world cinema. I remember being completely absorbed and drawn into the stories, despite the context being unfamiliar. That is why it is said that films transcend borders and emotions are universal.

When you were working as an actor, did you ever have to struggle to find work?

ND: No, because acting was never an ambition and therefore there was no particular goal to struggle for! When you have a specific destination in mind, you work towards it despite the challenges and struggles. You are driven by it. I have always seen my work as part of a continuous journey of self-expression and sharing. This frees me from the fear of failure and having to prove myself. I still don't live the life of an actor, whatever that means!

Did your parents' opinions influence you in some way in selecting the subject of Firaaq *as your first film?*

ND: My parents have influenced me, but not in a conscious way. Their own commitment to a more inclusive world has helped me question our prejudices and biases, which in some ways is the theme of *Firaaq*. They raised me with a lot of freedom to choose, and while they do share their thoughts, I don't think I have been 'told' what to do. In any case, *Firaaq* was not a conscious choice. It was a story I wanted to tell as I felt compelled to respond to the growing divisiveness and violence around me.

I gave various drafts of the script to my mother to read and discussed her feedback in detail. I also took her help for the Gujarati dialogues that some of the characters in the film spoke.

What were your dreams when you were growing up?

ND: I had many dreams and they kept changing! I learnt Odissi for twelve years and wanted to be an Odissi dancer. Then there was a time that I met a dynamic IAS officer who made me want to be one too. When I learnt pottery, it was so therapeutic, I felt that I would be happiest being a potter. Subconsciously, very early on, I felt like I wanted to 'make a difference'. Maybe that's what drew me to street theatre when I was seventeen. I would even argue with my father about his profession as a painter and how I thought it didn't help the world. Later, I understood that art has the ability to dive deep into our subconscious, impacting our perceptions and responses. Creativity is not an elitist activity as it is often portrayed. Art has been there since the time of cavemen and women. Through the ages, it has been an important form of expression and engagement. No wonder art threatens the bigoted and they want to ban books and films and stop artists from mirroring society through their work.

What may have attracted you to cinema?

ND: I was always fascinated by how stories are told through an audio-visual medium. As a viewer, I see the power of cinema — it can trigger conversations, humanize the other, challenge prejudices, spark new ideas and expose inconvenient truths. Of course, not all cinema does that but good cinema, where the form and content are in sync, can slowly and subliminally create change. And as I see films as a means to an end, this has been the primary reason for me to engage with cinema. I do believe that stories are what touch people and people change when they are moved.

Did the voice that you can direct come from within you or outside?

ND: To want to direct and have the confidence of jumping into the process can only come from within. It helped when eminent directors like Mrinal Sen, Mani Ratnam and Deepa Mehta told me that I should direct. Perhaps, also because I was equally interested in everything that was happening on the set. It could also have been their way of shutting me up [*laughs*]. On a serious note, I have always been interested in other aspects of film-making beyond acting. But more than all that, it was an inner desire to be a storyteller through a medium I was familiar with and exposed to.

How did you meet the producer of your first film as a director?

ND: I had gone to Cannes in 2007. I showed the script of *Firaaq* to some producers I met there and to Gilles Jacob, the then president of the Cannes Film Festival. He asked me to meet a producer who had just left Cannes. He thought she was fantastic and that we would be a good fit for each other. So, I went to Paris and met her. She loved the script and instantly agreed to produce it. I went back and jumped right into the pre-production. A couple of months later, when I was on my way to Karlovy Vary Film Festival (Czech Republic) to be a part of the jury, I passed through Paris as she wanted me to meet her husband/business partner. I met her husband and was shocked by how obnoxious he was [*laughs*]. Without much ado, he started talking money in the crassest terms. When I asked him to draw up a contract, he aggressively declined and retorted, 'Why do you want a contract? If we can have faith in you without you doing anything before, who are you to ask for a contract from a big company like ours!'

I was aghast and his wife, who looked very uncomfortable, did not intervene. While I was losing a good budget for my passion project, I knew this was not the producer I wanted, so I told him I didn't want to work with him.

I was understandably upset when I reached Karlovy Vary Film Festival and impulsively decided that I would only work with an Indian producer. On my return, a friend and film-maker, Rahul Dholakia, introduced me to Shailendra Singh of Percept Picture Company. When I met him, I told him, 'I am a first-time director, but I need to have the final cut. Also, I do not want anybody to interfere with my creative decisions whether that of cast or crew.' [*Laughs.*] To my surprise, Shailendra Singh agreed to everything. We signed the contract the next day.

What were some significant experiences and learnings from working with your first producer?

ND: It was only when I started the shoot that I realized how important a producer's role is. In India, producers often think that just being an investor suffices. I ended up having to do a lot of producing myself but I would not have learnt as much about the various aspects of production if things were not as they were. Since I had never assisted anyone or been trained formally, this learning was very precious to me.

Of course, I made many mistakes, and at that time I wanted to make a different, novel film and not just create a rendition of the ones that already existed. Now when I look back at my journey of *Manto*, I realize I ended up making some similar mistakes and some new ones!

As a young film-maker who has directed two films, what do you think a director brings to the table in creating and producing a film?

ND: First of all, I am not that young [*laughs*] and definitely not prolific, as I did my second film, *Manto*, ten years after my first.

When I started working as an actor, I realized it's the director who is the captain of the ship. It is their vision that is reflected in every department. The director has to make every choice, every decision during the film-making process and this impacts how the film will finally turn out.

I have often been asked what directors do. The cameraman shoots the scenes, the actor performs, the editor edits, songs are composed by the music director and so on. Everyone on the set is bringing their singular and unique talents or skills. And while it is a collaborative process, it is the director's vision that creates the alchemy needed to make a film. Can you imagine an orchestra without a conductor? In fact, in films, it's more than a conductor. It's not just the vision, but an involved director is hands-on in every department and works closely with every department. The director collaborates with every key cast and crew member to ensure what they have imagined is translated on to the screen. The director's work may seem invisible but plays a big part in the making of a film. The whole is, after all, more than the sum of its parts.

Please share with us a few insights as an actor-turned-director.

ND: Having worked on forty films as an actor, and now having directed both *Firaaq* and *Manto*, I can tell you that being an actor has helped in working with my cast but there is so much that goes into making a film, before and after the shoot. Direction is not only what happens in those thirty or forty-five days of shooting. In both my films, being an actor helped me greatly in communicating intent and specific instructions to the cast. I have worked with a wide range of actors—eminent film actors, theatre practitioners and complete novices facing the camera for the first time—and my work was made easier by knowing the feeling of being on the other side of the camera. My actors have often said that they felt more understood and could communicate better with an 'actor–director'. I am sure similar advantages would be felt by a cinematographer–director with regards to the technicalities of visualizing a film.

Share with us some insights into the actor–director relationship, from your first experience directing actors on Firaaq?

ND: I never told my actors, 'See, the camera is here and you adjust your positions and movements according to it.' This, I learned from my first film, *Fire*, with Deepa Mehta. She would do the basic blocking and then provide the actors the space to do what came naturally to them. After experiencing this, I decided that if I have a different way in which I want them to perform, I would share my thoughts and we could organically come to a consensus. Usually, the actor is convinced of any changes I want to implement as they trust that I understand the larger vision of the film better, having lived with it for longer. I always aim to be a willing listener as it is a collaborative process.

Firaaq had seasoned actors like Naseeruddin Shah, Paresh Rawal, Raghubir Yadav and Deepti Naval. Yet, the interaction and collaboration with each one of them was distinctly unique. Their personalities are different and so is their acting process. Actors like Nawazuddin Siddiqui and Shahana Goswami were comparatively new to the medium at the time but there was no lack of instinctive talent and commitment in the cast. After the shoot, Naseeruddin Shah sent me a message saying, 'I was impressed with your precise and clear instructions.' That's a compliment I treasure as it comes from a very critical person! [*laughs*].

What kept you going those ten years, beyond acting?

ND: Directing, for me, has not been a part of any design. It is a means to respond to what goes on around me as well as to share my concerns and interests. I had no plans of directing any film after *Firaaq*. In the last ten years, I was busy with many things—I wrote, directed and performed a play called *Between the Lines*. I was the chairperson of the Children's Film Society for three years (which I probably took more seriously than I needed to!). I was selected as one of the sixteen World Yale Fellows, and had several speaking engagements. I also wrote a monthly column for the *Week* for eight years and, of course, was busy raising my son. I have become quite skilled at juggling several things simultaneously—like most women! It was only after forty films, twenty years of being on the fringes of the film industry, and four years of research and writing that I felt equipped, both emotionally and creatively, to tell Manto's story.

What was your earliest memory of reading Manto's story and your first impression of him? Does that impression persist on revisiting his life as a director of his biopic?

ND: I first read Manto when I was in college and was struck by his simple yet profound narrative. I bought the five-volume collection called *Dastavez* in Devanagari. But I only read some of his short stories. It was only in 2012, during his centenary celebrations, that I rediscovered Manto. That is also when I read his essays that told me a lot more about the man behind the writer.

For years, I nursed the idea of making a film based on Manto's stories, even before *Firaaq*. But the story of his life took almost six years to be made. I needed to feel equipped, both emotionally and creatively, to tell this story that needed to be told. I realized I could not make a film about the writer without showing glimpses of his writings; they were inseparable. Therefore, I chose to integrate some of the stories that had left a deep impression on me in his narrative. Just as in his story, the line between fact and fiction is blurred, so in the film too, his narrative is interspersed with stories that he wrote.

What for you is the relevance of Manto today?

ND: Over the six-year journey of making the film, the relevance of Manto in contemporary times has only grown. We are still grappling with issues of freedom of expression and struggles of identity—our identities remain inextricably linked to caste, class and religion as opposed to the universality of human experience. Manto was relevant in his time and will continue to be relevant for a long time to come.

Today, we can see censorship in many forms—institutional censorship, the self-proclaimed custodians of culture, and artists and writers who are self-censoring out of fear. Manto fought for the right to tell the truth—unvarnished and undiluted. Therefore, he is very inspirational.

For me, making *Manto* was not just about Manto, the man, but invoking the *Mantoiyat* ('Mantoness')—the desire to be outspoken and free-spirited—that I believe all of us have, whether dormant or awakened. I think people will see themselves more honestly after watching his journey.

Is it important for a new director to pick up skills to direct actors? Would knowing the basics of acting help develop such 'skills'?

ND: I think learning about acting is a good idea; however, to be a director, it is advantageous to learn about every aspect of film-making. It is important for the director to understand actors and consider them as people first, rather than as just talent. The director must gain an insight into the actors' vulnerabilities, strengths and shortcomings. Some actors work best when they feel a little edgy and therefore like being pushed, whereas others might just crumble if you do that. The director must be aware of their self-esteem, not in a manipulative way, but in a gentle, empathetic way. It is both a craft and an instinct for a director to understand the actors and how they work best.

A director must understand that the actors need to make the characters their own in order to play them convincingly. The final performance seen on-screen is an outcome of this collaboration. Therefore, sometimes it is difficult to gauge how much of it is the actor's performance and how much is the director's interpretation and vision. And this is true of almost every department.

As an actor, what would you be possibly looking for in a new director to agree to being cast in their film?

ND: It is a fine balance between the director giving me the freedom to interpret the character in the way I understand it and the director's larger vision of the film. An actor cannot possibly have complete knowledge of the evolution of their character, and therefore it is important that the director must have a clear vision of the story and the character's arc. At times, there might be a difference of opinion but the director must be able to convince the actor of their intent or else be open to other interpretations. Together, the idea is to make the characters authentic and true to the vision of the story.

Sometimes, many people who are starting out new are simply networking in a shallow way, building a CV without really absorbing anything along the way, not realizing some other elements about their work are more important to get that elusive first break.

ND: The first question that a director must ask is: what is the real reason for them to tell their story? Only an honest intention can give birth to an honest piece of art. If they are distracted by more worldly or shallow reasons, more often than not, the film will reflect this. If I sense this in a new director when they come to pitch their story to me, I usually decline their offer. Also, new directors must understand that cinema is not a science but an art. There are no equations, permutations and combinations that can explain this alchemy.

'Cinema is alchemy', that's truly interesting, could you please elaborate?

ND: Unlike chemistry, which is defined and exact, alchemy is a vaguer art. It refers to a practice where you mix five ingredients and do not necessarily get the expected result from the mixture.

You can mix the same ingredients over and over again and get a different result each time. Similarly, in a film, you cannot put one spoon each of emotion, performance, action, comedy and romance, and expect it to be a huge hit every time. Here, we are not even talking about a good or bad film (if such things exist), but about how a lot of mainstream directors and producers think they know the formula for success and yet we know that it doesn't work that way. For every successful film, there are many that sink without a trace. Often independent films, too, suffer when they think there is a formula to get nominated in film festivals or get awards. The alchemy works only when you honestly and creatively tell a story.

The same applies to pottery. Take glazing for example: you may think, 'I want to paint the exterior green, edges white and interiors blue.' The fascinating and exciting part of glazing, just as in cinema, is that the result will not be what you imagined it to be.

Any significant learning the actor in you realized only after you became a director?

ND: As an actor, one is often unaware of the dynamics and challenges on set. So much of what we perform is finally realized on the screen through the vision of the director, how it's shot and edited, the role of sound and music in enhancing or diminishing the characters . . . basically the director can make or break a character beyond the actor's performance. I also learnt that while an actor must ask questions, contribute and discuss their characters freely, they must also realize that actors have a limited knowledge of their character graph, as they tend to see it more in isolation. The director has a more holistic view of how each character plays out in relation to other characters and the story at large. That is why theatre is seen more as an actor's medium, and film, as the director's.

What were your experiences as a producer? Did you ever lose faith during the making of Firaaq?

ND: While I faced many challenges, I never lost faith in the fact that I wanted to tell this story. And that kept me going. At any given point, hundreds of factors needed to be dealt with and many simultaneous decisions needed to be made. I wanted to push the pre-production ahead by two months, but my DOP could not. During the shoot, there were ego clashes or disagreements and I had to be the harmonizing force. It was a lonely journey even though it was a collaborative project. At the end of a shooting day, while most can afford to relax, the director with a few key crew members continue to plan for the next few days. A director works twenty-four hours a day. Often, I could not sleep because I was so wired-up or troubled by the decisions I had taken during the day. At times, I felt like I had made compromises to keep the peace on set. I was upset with my weakness even though most people perceive me to be strong. I would ask myself why I gave in but in retrospect, I realized that having a conducive environment for my cast to perform was worth the sacrifice. For me, it was important to create and maintain a happy and safe space for everybody to bring out their best.

The challenges persisted right from the beginning through the post-production and release of the film. But now, when I look back, I see it as one of my biggest learning curves. I enjoyed every phase of film-making, with all its trials and tribulations, and am grateful to all those who had faith in me and the story I wanted to tell.

Making *Firaaq* pushed my boundaries, and not just creatively. In fact, after *Manto*, I feel that directing films is a deeply impactful, emotional and spiritual journey. You get to know so much about yourself and how you respond to different situations and different people. It helped me grow as a person and a film-maker.

Is a director, particularly a first-time director, supposed to have all the answers?

ND: The short answer is no! A friend and director advised me before the shoot, 'The only tip I can give you is that you are the leader and everybody needs to look up to you. Your cast and crew are going to ask you many questions. As a first-time director, even if you do not know the correct answer, always tell them that you know, because people look up to you to instil confidence. If you need time to think about it, tell them you will get back to them. Never admit that you do not know.' I told my friend that I was surely not going to do that! The director is not supposed to know everything. Whether in my first film or my tenth, there will be things I would not know and that would be perfectly fine. But I would find out and make the best decision possible. In fact, a smart director would listen to all good suggestions and make the most informed choice. This may seem like a sign of weakness, but in fact, one needs strength to be open-minded in a field that is so deeply hierarchical.

As a child, you think your parents know everything. Over the years, you realize they actually don't. You accept your parents' vulnerability only when they admit, 'I do not know this, but wait, let me find out about it, or let us discover it together.' You end up respecting them more for that. Similarly, there have been occasions when I wanted to explore an idea by thinking aloud or asking a question. For instance, I was once asked on a shoot, 'Do you need a rifle, or a machine gun for this scene?' I admitted that I did not know the difference [*laughs*]. I went over the choices, understood the difference and then decided on the appropriate one for the scene. Why pretend to know when you don't? Even as an actor, I have never looked at my directors to have 'all' the answers. What I am looking for is simply the honesty to discover or unearth the answers, within or without me.

Another lesson I learnt, as a director, is that you can make all the possible promises and schedules, but life has her own plans! Your talents, technicians and weather gods have theirs too! How you deal with equanimity is the magic of directing. One does falter but I try to minimize it. No film-school degree can teach you this. Only film-making can.

They say film-making is a lot about letting go, especially during editing. Were you able to do it, especially as it was your first film?

ND: It's not easy! As a writer and director, I lived with the material for three years, passionately, making sure every little bit was the best it could be in terms of the crew, cast, locations and pre- and post-production. The danger in this is that one gets very attached to the minutest of things and sometimes you lose objectivity. But that's why collaborating with crew members helps in getting a different point of view.

For instance, there was a scene we shot in a hospital that needed more than a hundred junior artists. It was hard enough to find a hospital that would allow us to shoot in it, and, on top of which, the extras were not professionals. We somehow managed to get the scene we wanted. But when I watched the scene at the editing table, it felt like it wasn't helping the flow of the story. While the memory of the hardship of shooting the scene was still too fresh, I did want to omit it even though I had invested so much time, energy and money in it. I did not want to miss the woods for the trees, so finally, I told my editor, Sreekar Prasad, to get rid of it. He looked at me surprised, and said, 'I too wanted to edit it out but did not have the heart to tell you, knowing how much you had endured to shoot it. It is tough to convince a director to get rid of something, especially when she is also the writer. And that too, doing it all for the first time!'

You seem to have been able to let go quite easily, what was your inspiration?

ND: Sardar Gurcharan Singh, whom we all lovingly called Daddy-ji, the pioneer of studio pottery in India, was a huge inspiration in letting go. I got my first pottery lesson from him as he was very close to my father. I loved my little creations on the wheel, however crooked they were. Daddy-ji would cut each pot with the cutting thread to check if the walls of the pots were getting more even. Slowly, they became better and at one point, I was tempted to save a little pot and asked him if I could not cut it. Daddy-ji burst into his very childlike laugh and said, 'Let go . . . You will make many more. Never get too attached to your pots.' That important lesson has stayed with me since then. Whenever I struggle with the conflicting emotion of letting go, I remember his words. In fact, in *Manto*, I was able to do a lot more of it. Adopting this philosophy helped me, not just in writing and editing, but throughout the shoot.

In 1987, while still in college, I made my first film [a documentary] on Daddy-ji, at the behest of my father who said, 'Make it before it is too late, or no one will know of his great contribution to pottery.' As I adored him myself, I took up the challenge without knowing anything about films. This furthered my love for Daddy-ji, pottery, and all that he stood for.

You made a documentary before you made Firaaq? *How must that experience have helped you later as a director?*

ND: In between, I also made public service ads—a ninety-second one on rainwater harvesting and three sixty-second ones on education. Initially, I was unsure about how I would convey a message in an interesting way in such a short a time, but I soon realized that every format has its own strengths and challenges. The documentary and these shorts helped me understand the technical aspects and the work that goes into making a film before and after the shoot, which, as an actor, I was not privy to.

How did you come to choose a socio-political subject for your first film?

ND: Since the Gujarat riots of 2002, every time I went to that state, I returned with a heavy heart. Moreover, the conversations all around, whether personal or in the media, were getting increasingly polarized. There were people who were even justifying the violence and that was deeply troubling. It was the first time I saw live video images of a riot as NDTV had become the first 24/7 channel.

I decided to hold several talks after that and called them 'Identity and the Notion of the "Other"'. But this didn't seem enough. As I had access to the medium of cinema, I decided to share my concerns through a film that would reach a larger audience.

Violence spares nobody and I wanted to show this without showing any violence in the film. I am troubled by the way violence is often normalized, if not glorified, in cinema, even if the intent is to the contrary. I wanted to explore the lingering psychological impacts of violence and that is why I set *Firaaq* in the aftermath of the carnage. While I chose this socio-political backdrop, I was clear that I wanted the narrative to be told through intimate, human stories.

For me, the film was only a medium and not an end in itself. I didn't choose *Firaaq*, it was part of no design. In fact, had I done it as more of a deliberate progression, I would have chosen subjects that were easier to handle. But *Firaaq* allowed me to respond to my own despair and discomfort with what was happening around me. I would say the same, even more, for *Manto*.

Who was your DOP? Why did you select him?

ND: Ravi K. Chandran. To tell a story well, it is equally important that the form and its craft are handled with the minutest care by the best crew. I was neither trained in a film school nor on a film set, so I wanted to get an experienced cinematographer to help me with the visualization of the film. I had done the rainwater harvesting PSA and two films as an actor with Ravi K. Chandran. He, too, was keen to work with me again and said yes without even reading the script. I told him, 'Ravi, do it for the right reasons and not because we are friends.' After reading the script, he called and said, 'Now I am doing the film because of the script more than for you!' I had worked with many other cameramen on the thirty films I had been a part of until that point, so I did have options, and many of them had even expressed their interest in shooting my first film as a director. I chose to work with Ravi because I liked his work and he brought a special enthusiasm to the project.

What was your general process working with your DOP?

ND: As I had written the script and had spent three years working on every aspect of it, I could almost 'see' the film before we began the shoot. Ravi brought a lot to the table, and together we decided on the look and feel of the film. He also helped me understand the technicalities.

I wanted each of the stories to be shot differently and yet have a cohesive visual language. For instance, Hanif and Muneera's story (played by Nawaz and Shahana) needed to be handheld. I wanted it to have a kind of nervous and edgy feel. For Khan Saab and Kareem's story (Naseeruddin Shah and Raghubir Yadav), we decided on using the tracks and trolley to give it a more classical and fluid feel. Arti and Sanjay's story (Deepti Naval and Paresh Rawal) needed more bare and static imagery and therefore the camera too was more locked down, with no movement. Ravi and I discussed this, and more, in great detail. We visualized the film in a way that, we felt, would be best for its ensemble structure.

Were you confident or nervous on your first day? What was it like?

ND: My first day was not very different from my tenth! There was so much to do and take care of that there was no time to be nervous. My unit, while very supportive, was not fully confident of this first-time 'female' director, who was still perceived as an actress. Many probably thought that Ravi, the experienced cameraman, would call the shots. Luckily, by the end of the day, they knew that they did have a director on set!

I had planned the first day with Naseer and Raghubir, as they were both friends I'd known for years. However, this didn't ensure a smooth start like I'd hoped it would. Naseer, who was to arrive a day before the shoot, arrived the next morning due to some delays on his previous set. He was late and in a bad temper! I wanted my set to be a calm and happy place. I definitely didn't want an edgy start, so I told Naseer that he could take some time to cool down even though we were all waiting on set. Thankfully, by the time he came back, he had calmed down and apologized.

I think you earn respect by simply doing your job well and with integrity. You have to treat your actors and crew at a humane level, not just as professionals. When you take them with you, it should not be just because of where they are on the ladder of hierarchy, but because of who they are as people.

New directors may get overwhelmed by the fear of not being well-versed with the technical aspects of cinematography. How did you feel about this?

ND: Having conceived, written and lived with the script for years, I knew the spaces and the characters, and I was able to tell Ravi exactly what I wanted. The position of the camera and the choice of lens were guided by the visual in my head. I could see if the character needed to be in close-up or viewed from afar. For me, the form is always guided by the content. For instance, if it was a very intense moment for a character, I knew I would want a close-up.

A new director, who does not have knowledge of camera techniques, need not get bogged down by the lack of it. We have made technicalities look more fearful and important than they really are. They are tools, important ones, but as a director, you do not need to know all of them. As long as the vision is clear and personal, that is enough to guide you and your cinematographer.

How did you select the editor? What was the process of working with him?

ND: I was fortunate to have Sreekar Prasad, one of the most eminent editors in India. He has edited many films, including a film I acted in. I admired his work and liked his temperament.

Sreekar is very open to other ideas and gives his own opinion emphatically. In times of disagreement, he understands that it is finally the director's vision that guides the process. I noticed, during the film-making process, that everyone was making their own film in their head! I think this assertion of their own versions occurs when they are dealing with a first-time director and more so if that director happens to be a woman. But Sreekar was understanding, willing to listen and try out different things.

He was in Chennai, so I would travel to see and discuss the edit. Twice, my producer paid for my stay in Chennai, but every time I saw the edit, I felt it needed more work. Fortunately, we became such good friends that I would stay at his house and so I could afford more trips. His wife would make delicious meals and we would work in the editing room opposite his house. He would assemble the rushes, do a first pass on the edit and send it to me. I would then make my notes and send them back. There were several such interesting back-and-forth. He's also somebody I definitely wanted to work with again, and so I got him for my second film as well! But I didn't realize that long-distance editing would be really challenging with a child to take care of. I could not make the numerous trips to Chennai. However, editing remains my favourite part of the film-making process. After the shoot I feel like I didn't get what I really wanted. But the process of editing gives you back the confidence as you see the film slowly come together.

Does the job of a director also involve ego-management skills?

ND: It's not just ego management, it's constant people management that one ends up doing. That said, nobody can teach or prepare you to handle people's egos or the politics on set. Human psychology has always fascinated me. There is an interesting book on it I had read, *Games People Play*. Not that reading it helped me much! But I believe if you genuinely engage with people, they do the same.

A director is like a parent. When egos between crew members, talents or technicians flare up, you have to sit them down and help them communicate. In most cases, it is just a breakdown in communication. The director needs to always keep their cool because even in the most stressful situation, you cannot walk off your own set [*laughs*]. The fact that you cannot do that is such a great learning process, a great way to put your own ego to the test. That is what you learn through directing—how to handle people, their egos, and sometimes, your own too.

Did you ever have to take the fall for mistakes that weren't necessarily yours as the director?

ND: Of course! But that is something directors need to do. It comes with being a parent! If something went wrong with the shoot, it definitely came to me as I became the default producer on set. The funny thing was that when anything beyond our control went wrong, somebody from the crew would be quick to comment, 'This happened because you do not believe in God and don't break the customary coconut before the first shot of each day!' I never stopped the crew from following their traditions but was sure that I did not want to partake in such superstition. I had to bear the responsibility for everything that went wrong.

Who were the unsung heroes of your film?

ND: In most films, the light men and spot boys are the least acknowledged, even though they work the hardest on shoots. They are the first ones to come and the last ones to leave. On the first day of the shoot, in the beginning of my impassioned speech to my crew, I first acknowledged my light men. They carry heavy lights, risk their lives by climbing precariously placed ladders and working with unsecure electrical wirings. Producers, often, do not secure their working conditions, although now, things are changing. I know of an incident when a light boy fixing lights at a great height fell and died. All the producer did was to pay his family a meagre sum of Rs 20,000.

The spot boys, too, are the unsung heroes. I remember that some of the spot boys got so attached to the child actor, they cried on the last day of his shoot. As an actor, you value the spot boys even more, as you see them taking care of the cast and crew with such dedication. But as a director, you realize the worth of every single person, every single profession, technician and talent. Some are more invisible than others and that's why you need to give them even more credit. As film is a collaborative art, one cannot undermine anyone's contribution, as each person plays a unique and necessary role. It is as much their film as it is the director's and that of the 'stars'. It is important to give them that sense of ownership. The gap between the most privileged and least will remain, the least the director/producer can do is ensure that the gap is minimal. My executive producers used to remind me that this was not my job and I should stop distracting myself with making the set more egalitarian. But for me, it is not only important to make a different kind of film, but also to make it differently. I have to say, I was more successful in my efforts in *Firaaq* than I was in *Manto*. This was probably because the latter was a much bigger project with too many things to do and too many cooks stirring the broth. I do hope that in my next film, I can focus on things behind the scenes as much as I would like to.

What are the perks of being a first-time director, which a director may never have the privilege of having again?

ND: It is akin to growing up. A child's first-time experience of everything he or she stumbles upon and discovers is with a sense of awe. Similarly, as a first-time director, the magic of every phase of the film-making process has a sense of wonderment that you never experience in the same way again.

When you do films thereafter, there will be some small, new discoveries and wonders, but not the ones that can happen only once. Each film will be different, but your first-time encounters will always remain special!

If your child were eighteen today, and came up to you and said, 'I want to be in films. I want to be a director.' What would you tell them?

ND: Firstly, I would ask my child why he wants to direct. I would encourage him to ask himself why he wants to undertake this journey. If I feel that the reasons are genuine and not dictated by the glamourized perception of film-making, I would sit him down, talk about his reasons and then support him.

I would ask him what stories he is feeling compelled to tell and why. I would tell him that the best expression comes from observing life and people. I would ask him to be more open to exposing himself to truths and experiences that may not be from his immediate world; to travel, read and engage with people and their stories.

I would probably give him the advice that I, myself, have not followed! Such as, assisting a director he admires, going to film school and watching more diverse films. I would not give him very specific instructions as he has to discover his own path. And as mentioned before, there is no science to this or rules to follow. I would want him to find his own voice, and assure him that the rest usually falls in place. While it sounds contradictory, sometimes paying attention to small things in life can help you navigate through the bigger ones. This can be applied to both film-making and life.

What are some of the most special things you feel you are blessed with, being in this profession, and being a director?

ND: Making and being in films has given me a wider platform to share my concerns and connect with the world around me. Being a director has given me the opportunity to tell stories that matter to me. When I started working, I was engaged with grassroots-level NGOs. It expanded my understanding of the human condition beyond my own world. Without those experiences, I could not have made the most of the platforms I have access to today, whether as an actor or director. It is my experience with social work and advocacy that helped me in portraying characters and articulating the stories in my films.

The subjects I pursued in my films were heavily influenced by my experience in social work. Having found a new and larger platform through acting and directing, my voice is able to reach more people. From grassroots-level social work, I realized my work was finding its way into the realm of social advocacy. Because I'm a part of the film industry, various forums invite me to speak. I take these opportunities to share my concerns and engage with issues of social justice and human rights.

In the beginning, I was uncomfortable with my role as a social advocate as I knew that I was being invited because of my newfound 'celebrity' status. There were many others who were far more engaged in those issues and thus more qualified to do justice to the speaking engagements. Over the years, I have made peace with it by realizing that I might as well use these platforms to be a catalyst for dialogue on important issues and the people who have dedicated their lives to them. In fact, I am mindful of my unique position of straddling the edge of these two worlds, human rights and films, simultaneously. Though often the film industry thinks of me as an activist and the social sector views me as a film person, I have learnt not to put myself in either of the boxes.

My exposure to these completely distinct worlds has contributed to my growth and understanding of life and films in more ways than would have been possible if I had just chosen one. It has opened many doors that I would not have encountered, such as writing columns, speaking engagements in universities and various important conferences, festivals (both literary and film), fellowships like those at Yale and Harvard, among others. I would never have imagined that I would be showing *Firaaq* at Professor Amartya Sen's class at Harvard and, at the same time, would be invited to address a huge gathering of more than 10,000 rural women in a small town in the district of Anantpur, Andhra Pradesh.

I now believe that being a part of these two worlds has enriched my life greatly. In fact, I have come to the conclusion that specialization is overrated or, at the very least, not the right fit for me. Though my path may seem meandering, it has given me a greater sense of purpose and fulfilment. The lines between my life and work are very blurred and I like it that way!

PERSPECTIVE FROM ANOTHER LENS

Cinematographer Ravi K. Chandran speaks of Nandita Das

My elder brother [Ramachandra Babu] is a cinematographer. The age gap between us is seventeen years, so, I grew up in an environment where actors visited us and I visited film sets. My first break as a cinematographer came while I was assisting a senior cameraman on the set of Mani Ratnam's second film *Unaru* (1984). Mani sir asked me to shoot a scene that seemed a bit complicated; however, I managed to do it in record time and quite well. I am a naturally restless person and I have made a variety of choices to keep myself on my toes and be inventive in my career.

I've known Nandita since her early years as an actor. We met on the sets of a Mani Ratnam film. Over the years, we became friends and she'd tell me that if she ever directed a film, she would like me to shoot it. When she approached me with the script of

Firaaq, I didn't just empathize with the nature of the subject but also gathered from our initial interactions that she cared deeply for the people who suffered in the Godhra riots (2002). The film does not have any scenes depicting the riot or the gruesome rapes and killings, yet she, and her writer, had managed to create and maintain the tension and dynamic of the riots. By the use of sound, lighting and dialogue, she created an atmosphere that showed how deeply it was impacted by hatred and the police's neglect of the victims' genuine concerns for their lives and property.

We decided the look of the film during pre-production. We shot the stories of the various characters in different lenses. The portions of Nawaz were shot with a handheld camera, because we wanted it to be edgy with a lot of nervous energy. We shot Naseeruddin's portions with a wide lens of 16 mm to make sure that you could see a lot of his environment. For Paresh's portions, we lit very bright and flat and used the wide lenses to portray his non-emotional state. We shot Deepti Naval's portion with a shallow depth of field to bring the viewer in close proximity to her trauma. Moreover, we used different film stocks for these characters because they were so different from each other and we wanted the audience to register these differences in their worlds subconsciously. Each individual's story in the film has a different visual texture to it. These were very good decisions Nandita made as director. She surprised me many times in the making of her first film; I had perhaps expected less but she was on the top of her game as a director, extracting fine performances from seasoned actors such as Naseeruddin Shah, Deepti Naval and even a newbie like Nawazuddin Siddiqui. Her experience as an actor helps her stage scenes. For first-time directors, particularly, staging a scene can be a challenge. She understands the dynamics between the natural physicality of her characters, the camera angle [placement] and the movement of the actors in the three-dimensional space in front of the camera. Her characters gel in the space and the world they inhabit because of her own vast experience as an actor.

One of the scenes in *Firaaq* that I felt she directed very well was the one where the interfaith couple was shown in their house with their relatives. There were four characters in the scene and a very engaging discussion amongst them about the couple's decision to leave the city for fear of becoming the targets of religious hate and violence.

Nandita also made a wise choice about the make-up and costumes of the actors that made them seem like real characters from our lives and not fictional. From her own life and work experiences, she made a realistic film, which was important because it was based on a true event. Though the film was shot in Hyderabad, it seemed to be located in Gujarat, where the riots had taken place. Nandita later told us how Danny Boyle had appreciated the scene where Nawaz is chased by a cop at night on the streets while he is escaping with the child.

Honestly, there was no budget to shoot this scene the way it could have been, because the budget for the film was quite low, yet we managed to do a good job, if I do say so myself. Till the morning of the first day of the shoot, we were not certain if we would receive the necessary funds to make the film and she was ready to return to Mumbai without canning a single shot, but the funds arrived just in time for us to stick to our production schedule. I had managed to get the team of *Ghajini* (2008) to shoot our film at a very reasonable rate and with minimal equipment.

Nandita is really good in shooting realistic subjects but I think she'll be equally great in shooting a relationship drama. I hope she makes one someday soon.

She was very stressed during the making of this film because of the lack of adequate funds and it being her first film as a director. But I think she captained the ship commendably. There were times I was irritated and frustrated by the lack of experience of a few crew members and we clashed, but it's the job of the cinematographer to make peace and let work progress. At times, the editor, Sreekar Prasad, became a balancing force between my creative ego, which told me to stand by my convictions, and

Nandita's vision as the director. I managed to find a way to do this without sacrificing content. Years later, when I directed my first film, I realized how challenging it would've been for Nandita and the other first-time directors I had worked with. I began to see them in a new and better light thereafter.

Particularly for a first-time director, the cinematographer is perhaps the only other person on set that they can lean on when they feel nervous, intimidated or uninformed about something. That is why I think the director and cinematographer's relationship is considered a very critical and close one. The one common quality in the best directors I have worked with is their ability to be open to suggestions not only from their key crew but even from junior assistants. Nandita has this quality in her. She sincerely listens to and considers everyone's suggestions, including mine.

Another quality I've observed in Nandita and any good director is their ability to make me want to give them my best by treating me and other crew members and technicians as close associates. Even when she discusses a plot point with her team of assistants she makes sure to include me in the discussion and asks for my opinion. She is inclusive in her approach. If she was not certain about something she would ask me how I would shoot it to solve the issue. For me, direction means your ability to direct every department of film-making to help you tell your story most effectively. I think Nandita does a good job at that.

A moment between us, a personal moment, that I cherish is when Nandita met my wife. She told her, '[. . .] Hema, you are a lucky woman to be married to Ravi. Ravi often talks about you and speaks fondly of you. Few married men do that.'

SHAKUN BATRA

'A good producer understands that good direction is not just about what the director does between "action" and "cut". You must know how to utilize the producer's financial resources and the talents and energy of the actors and crew, and make them feel secure.'

FILMOGRAPHY

Ek Main Aur Ekk Tu (2012); *Kapoor & Sons* (2016)

SNEAK PEEK

Shakun Batra was born in Delhi and began acting in junior school. He was an assistant director in school plays since Class XI and directed the plays he wrote from Class X till his graduation. He studied at St Stephen's College. It was during a lecture in his college by TVC film-maker Tarsen Singh that he confided in his friend that he wanted to be a director someday. This was the first time he considered film-making as a career. Photography was his first love and he attended a film programme at Vancouver Film School, Canada, in 2004–05, where he also attended extra classes for cinematography. He worked in the TV-advertisement business for three months until his first film, *Don* (2006), where he was the assistant director, working under Farhan Akhtar.

MY TAKE

When I met Shakun Batra for this interview, he confessed, 'I am honoured that you asked me to be a part of your book, but I do not come anywhere close to some of the great film-makers you have onboard. Additionally, I am just one-film-old!' I told him, 'People consider my father a legend in film song-writing. Thanks to that, I was introduced to some renowned people in the film industry, since I began my career in 1999. I have worked with some excellent film-makers, in the past decade, in various creative capacities. I've pitched my scripts to many big producers. Yet, I am not even one-film old. Whereas, you've worked less than a decade in this profession and do not come from a family that is a part of this industry, still, you have made a film. That too a film produced by one of the best producers and having a terrific cast. I think that sure is an achievement in this complex business.'

Shakun is an enthusiastic and passionate person. Post our first meeting at a coffee shop, he asked me if I'd like to come to his house; however, I only had a few minutes to spare. He said he wanted to show me his collection of books on film that had inspired him. I agreed. Once we were there, he went on to tell me how some books and film-makers had influenced him. I was touched by his concern for me to write a better book and his generosity to share his sources of inspiration.

He volunteered to come to my house for the interview, as his own was under renovation. When he arrived, he gave me his digital audio recorder to use as a recording device to interview the other directors for this anthology. Such was his generosity and interest in the nature of my book. After I watched *Kapoor & Sons*, my beliefs were reaffirmed—we are flawed beings, we will have differences with each other but that we can be together, eventually, in spite of our shortcomings. With love arrive the twins: empathy and forgiveness. If we employ love in the detailing of our daily lives, the bigger picture will eventually turn out to be beautiful.

Shakun is not just a movie-lover, he is earnest in his love for film-making. He was bound to make it as a film-maker, I thought happily, as I drove away from his 'home of books' on cinema.

THE CONVERSATION

Rakesh Bakshi: Thank you for being a part of our book. Tell us a bit about where you were born. Where did you complete your schooling and college?

Shakun Batra (SB): Before we proceed, I must admit to you, once again, that I am surprised that you considered me for this anthology. After all, I am just one-film young! So, I consider it an honour, and I am indeed humbled, to be anywhere in this book. Thank you.

I was born in New Delhi. After my MA from Delhi University, I went to Vancouver Film School, Canada, for a basic course in film-making. Thereafter I returned to Delhi and later shifted to Mumbai. Earlier, I would tell my mom 'I am coming home' when I was travelling to Delhi. Now when I say 'I am heading home', she knows I mean Mumbai.

What are your fondest memories of your twenty-one years in Delhi?

SB: I grew up Adarsh Nagar, where everyone knew everyone. There were small shops in our neighbourhood that were known by their owner's names, for example, '*Vinod uncle ki video library*' [Vinod uncle's video library] or '*Batra uncle ki stationery ki dukaan*' [Batra uncle's stationery shop]. I look back at my school life with nostalgia. Schooldays were fun. I was engaged in loads of extracurricular activities. My school had music and theatre festivals, in which I took part enthusiastically.

I studied in a Hindi-medium school till Class VII. Strangely, from Class VIII onwards, we were suddenly expected to speak in fluent English because the medium of instruction changed.

It was terrible! Thankfully, both my sisters were studying in an English boarding school, so they helped me learn the language.

Then I got into St Stephen's College, Delhi University, where everybody spoke in English. In school, we used to speak in English only when we were trying to be cool. But at Stephen's, English was the way of communicating with our peers and teachers, because of the diverse student body, not all of whom could speak in or understand Hindi. For me that was a shock and it took me a while to work on my English-language skills.

For a director like me, who is also writer (I've co-written my first two films with Ayesha DeVitre), these are two different faculties—thinking in Hindi and English and making a Hinglish film. However, because I have studied both the languages, I have a little advantage here. I can choose to think things out—particularly expressions or even complete scenes—in Hindi or English. This is a great boon for me or for that matter, any writer–director—to be able to switch from one language to another subconsciously and effortlessly.

I have lived in Mumbai for nearly eleven years now, and can clearly distinguish between Delhi Hindi and Mumbai Hindi. I can get into these spaces and the nuances of the characters' milieu pretty easily. This helps in creating realistic characters and consequently, believable dialogue. I love Delhi humour and films that reflect it. Films like *Khosla ka Ghosla* and *Oye Lucky! Lucky Oye!* remind me of my childhood, especially my neighbours in Adarsh Nagar. My Delhi uncles and aunties talk just like that. There has been a strong Punjabi influence in my life, which has naturally seeped into my script for *Kapoor & Sons*.

As a child did you read a lot?

SB: No. And my biggest handicap even today is that I read only books on films. I began reading these books when I started getting interested in film-makers and cinematographers.

Considering film books were your first introduction to film-making, what do you think about reading books in general?

SB: I think reading only one kind of book is problematic. When I read that Woody Allen, my favourite director, was influenced by Hemingway and Kafka, I wished I had read as much fiction too. It's not the same with movies though. I knew what kind of movies I wanted to watch early on. But when I go to a bookshop, I'm lost. I don't know what to pick up, which genre or writers to read. I have never been able to cultivate reading as a hobby nor found my genre as a reader.

So, I make up for what I feel is my shortcoming by watching lots of movies and exposing myself to different photographers. These are my two alternatives to reading for the necessary exposure I miss out on. I am always looking for and looking at still images and watching movies that are not part of the mainstream. I have exposed myself to other forms of art to try and compensate for not being a big reader of non-film books.

What is your earliest memory of a film that impressed you as a child?

SB: The first movie I became a fan of was *Haathi Mere Saathi*. I love animals. When Rajesh Khanna throws that party and all the animals are invited and are dining, it made me wish I could be there with them! My parents had to explain it was a just movie, but even now, the scene where Rajesh Khanna beats up the elephant makes me cry. The thing about this film is that it is not about the animals even though that's what it seems like. It is actually about this man, the hero, who becomes somebody from a nobody, and the realization that his best friend is an elephant comes to him only when things fall apart. The same elephant, whom, sadly, he had once misunderstood and beaten.

Annie Hall (1977), directed by Woody Allen, is another film I remember watching when I was quite young. I watched it thrice, back to back! *The Graduate* (1967) and *Rushmore* (1998) are my all-time favourites. I can watch them again and again!

When did you first wonder 'how do they make movies'?

SB: Watching *Haathi Mere Saathi* was the first cinematic experience that made me wonder how they filmed the dining scene with all the animals and the hero. I thought about this for days—what was this place? How did things happen there?

When did you realize there is a job called 'film director'?

SB: In 2001, TVC film-maker Tarsen Singh came for a lecture to my college. I heard him talk about film-making as his passion and became really excited. I started to realize the value a director brings to a film. I realized the enormous effort made by a director to create a film.

I was already into photography by then and had a fair idea of how images were captured. I could see the difference between the works of Henri Cartier-Bresson and Sebastião Ribeiro Salgado or someone like Patrick Demarchelier. Films, for me, were about finding your identity via art and your work.

It was during Tarsen Singh's lecture that I realized that a director brings his personal voice to a film. And that's when I told my best friend, Karan, that I wanted to become a film director.

Did photography get you interested in moving images, movies? Any iconic images from your early years of watching movies?

SB: It was Bresson who got me interested in visual imagery way before I acquired an interest in movies. His iconic photograph of a man jumping over a puddle of water enthralled me. I also loved the photograph of a cyclist riding on the street below taken from the top of a spiral staircase. Salgado's *Migration* is still stuck in my head.

As for movies, I vividly remember the iconic *E.T.* (1982) poster of the bicycle against the moon. I also found the scenes where the three friends in *Dil Chahta Hai* (2001) are racing and when they are on a ship eating fish very aesthetic.

Which director's work in terms of images and content do you like?

SB: Woody Allen. His cinema, his stories are subjective. He doesn't take his identity as a film-maker very seriously. He believes that making films is what he needs to do and so he does it. He is an amazing writer and could probably churn out a script and a film every year. Most of whom he continues to work with are people he has been working with since his very first film! He talks about extramarital affairs with humour but he never forgets the seriousness of it, for example, a movie like *Hannah and Her Sisters* (1986) is funny and warm at the same time.

Considering photography was your first love, tell us about your interest in it during your college years.

SB: I borrowed my uncle's camera and began shooting pictures. I started by shooting birds around Delhi. Then I began to travel out of Delhi, to places like Agra, Vrindavan, and began to think of themes to shoot around, for example, underprivileged kids.

That is when I realized how much I loved photography. I loved being able to capture images, emotions, faces and I got thoroughly into it. I was exposed to photographers like Bresson and Salgado, who got me hooked on to photography.

So, photography and playing the guitar were the two things I thought about for a long time as potential careers. However, photography turned out to be a stronger urge and that is how I decided on my career as a cinematographer.

What else influenced you to study film-making or cinematography?

SB: *Dil Chahta Hai* (2001). When I was in college, I had to go to my dad's office daily because he wanted me to go to 'work'. But in this film, the characters dress up casually even for their offices.

This made me realize that film-making was possibly less uptight about dress codes and more chilled out. I started watching films with renewed excitement thereafter.

I was already into photography and began to feel a deep need to be part of the images I saw in some of these films. I don't know exactly what, but there was something about the movies that got me excited to be in them. That is when I decided to go to film school and give cinematography a shot.

What did you study to learn cinematography?

SB: I got a scholarship to study accounts and my dad was happy, thinking his son will do an MBA and become a CA. To be honest, this is something I, too, considered as a career choice. In retrospect, I realize I had always wanted to move far away from home as I felt I had stayed there too long. I wanted to find my own space, even if it were a business school. I applied to a business university in the US and won a scholarship.

However, my US visa got rejected twice! I was shattered, thinking I have to stay back home and join my father's business. That is when I picked up the camera and took to photography more earnestly. I was in a bad place and wanted to do something with photography to escape what was pulling me down. I started shooting still images randomly and began enjoying it.

Then came the day when I had to tell my parents that I did not want to pursue business; that I really wanted to discover my creative side. When I told Amma, my grandmother, I wanted to be a cameraman, she was worried because our family had a business background and might now be associated with wedding videographers!

I learnt my lesson and began using the term 'cinematographer' to placate my family. Thanks to this complex and impressive-sounding word, 'cinematography', I got to leave home and travel to Canada to educate myself in a skill I loved. After my visit to Canada I travelled a lot, something I thought was important.

Even if it is in Mumbai and Delhi, I walk around a lot. It takes a while to start observing things, beyond just seeing stuff. When you are in a different or unfamiliar place, you notice even the 'smallest' of things.

Your family was against you becoming a film-maker. What could be the way forward for someone finding their parents opposed to their career choice?

SB: I cannot really advise anyone. Everyone's circumstances are different. Moreover, I've only done one film. A lot of the choices you make are instinctive. I realized this when I heard a story about one of my favourite photographers. Bresson and a painter were sitting and the painter asked him, 'How is it that you press the camera button at that precise moment and not a second before or a second later?' Bresson replied, 'How is it that you used red for that inch of paint stroke and not an inch more or less?' The answer for both would be, 'instinctively'.

Somewhere in your gut you will *know* whether your career choice is right or wrong for you. You must ask yourself, 'Why am I really here? What am I really doing here?' and answer them honestly.

We apply to film schools with many expectations. What was your experience like, having studied in one?

SB: If you think while applying to a film school that you will come out as a 'director', you are wrong. For me, my film education provided immense exposure to the world of cinema. I had never seen so many good movies, never heard about half of the directors whose movies I was watching. Just being able to go in and watch a film directed by a world-renowned director one Sunday and watch the rest of his films over the same week was a revelation. However, any film school can only give you what you want to take from of it.

For me, directing is about handling people, getting work done without overstepping each other's boundaries. Cinema is an art form that is expensive and not individualistic. You got to have a team to direct—a cameraman, lighting people, actors. Just because you have gone to film school does not mean that you know how to handle people. That is something you learn only when you work with production houses and directors.

After film school, what was your first job in the film industry?

SB: My first paid job was working for Farhan Akhtar, as his assistant in *Don* (2006). I went to the office of Excel Entertainment, met a woman called Shamira, and said, 'I will do any job, I just want to work in the movies. I just graduated from film school; here is my resume.' Later, they called me and offered me the position of DA. It was Zoya Akhtar who offered me my first job in the movies.

DA means you are more of a personal assistant to the director. You take care of their creative meetings, make sure their lunch is there on time, get coffee and photocopies, etc. What is great about the job is that you spend nearly twenty-four hours with the director! So, you get to observe the director making crucial creative decisions at close quarters. For me, just to be able to talk to a director of Farhan's calibre was exciting. Moreover, it was his first film, *Dil Chahta Hai*, that had made me think of films and film-making!

What was your biggest takeaway from working as the DA for Don?

SB: Discipline. Farhan is so disciplined in the manner he divides his work and gives 100 per cent attention to every division of film-making, both on and off set. He carries all the little details in the back of his mind but when he gets down to working on any one link in the chain of film-making, he is fully focused only on that aspect. Hard work, focus and conviction are things you cannot learn from a book; these are the things I learnt by working with Farhan.

Sometimes you have to be bull-headed about your conviction as there are some things you believe staunchly in and don't want to compromise on. Sometimes you have to be open-minded to suggestions. It's a combination of both. Give everybody a chance to talk to you, allow them to tell you what they think because they, too, are a part of the collaborative process of film-making. But you have to remember your role as the director. It is you who compiles and brings all the elements together, giving them direction. Someone occupying such a pivotal role should have their own point of view. This is not to say that everyone does not play an important role, because they do. Technicians have a high value because their suggestions are very informed and helpful. Then you need the talent to know that you've received a great idea. No one person can give you solely good or perfect ideas. They may pitch ten ideas, of which only one or two will be good. The greatest people you work with are the ones who are not scared to share their ideas. These are the people who will not crib or feel resentful if only one of their twenty ideas is accepted and implemented. Karan Johar is one such person. Even though he is a producer, and immensely experienced as a writer and a director, he never, even once, forced me to accept his ideas. He didn't even crib if I did not accept them.

There are also some great TVC film-makers from whom I learnt a lot. For example, Ram Madhvani, Prakash Verma, who tell a story in a very short period of time, thirty seconds, sixty seconds, which can be quite intimidating. You need to have a certain control on the craft to be able to pull that off effortlessly.

What else did you experience on your first job that may have helped you later as a first-time director?

SB: My first job was with Excel Entertainment, as the director's assistant for *Don*. Then I was the second AD in Aamir Khan's *Jaane Tu Ya Jane Na* (2008) and that's when I met Imran [Khan] who was to someday become the male lead in my first film as director!

Then I did *Rock On!!* (2008), after which I was prepping for another Farhan Akhtar film called *A Voice in the Sky*, but it was shelved. I also worked on some commercials with a bunch of different directors. I soon began to feel confident enough to take a shot at becoming a director.

I had arrived in Mumbai when I was twenty-one and for the next four years, I got the opportunity to work as an assistant with directors such as Farhan Akhtar, Abhishek Kapoor and Abbas Tyrewala. I began to consciously ponder over what I should do in this industry and began to think of writing a script with the hope that I could direct it as my first feature.

You co-wrote your two first films. Did you write stories when you were younger?

SB: I used to write letters to my girlfriend. When I broke up with her, I must have written a few letters, some with poems, about my heartbreak. That was where my earliest 'writing' journey began and ended.

However, when I started writing my first script, *Ek Main Aur Ek Tu*, I began enjoying the process. I still do not think I am much of a writer, but nevertheless, I want to keep writing, even if it is to keep myself busy until the next film.

It is good if a director can write because the one thing he needs to understand is storytelling. If you have not done any amount of writing, you are like a commentator commenting on Sachin Tendulkar's strokes without having played the game yourself. When you have been through the process of writing, you understand the mind of the writer you work with. How a scene evolves, what are the layers in that scene, how does the scene unfold, what can you hold back, what can you give, is it getting boring, what is the subtext? These kinds of things come up during the creation of a script and you will only understand how to deal with them if you have been writing too. It is easy to point out the problems in a scene; however, it's not so easy to create solutions for them. When you try working it out yourself, you recognize the thought process and hard work that go into its creation. Sometimes a three-page scene is easier to write than a half-page one. Sometimes it is just about creating the correct subtext; writing the implicit dialogues.

I do not consider myself a writer but I would love to be able to continue to collaborate, write and be involved in this process. Writing helps me understand myself better, stirs up old memories.

I did not start writing *Ek Main Aur Ek Tu* with the intention of making a movie. It was my first script and since I was writing for the first time, I decided to go with instinct than conventional wisdom. I only had the characters in mind and it made sense to go with them. Over the one and a half years that we took to complete it, the change from my first draft to the draft I shot was pretty drastic, though the essence remained the same. My script got better as I went ahead and directed it, because I kept improvising things.

You co-wrote your first two films with Ayesha DeVitre. What do you think about the process of co-writing?

SB: I have become more conscious of the process of giving a part of myself to a script that is not completely mine. All the big directors I know of do not write their scripts, yet they have their unique signature on their films. I think, this happens by being able to put a part of you in the movie, and that is not necessarily always in the script alone. It is also about trying to be able to find a hook in the story you relate to and being able to tell the story through that perspective. You do not have to be a writer to be able to tell a story convincingly as a director.

Considering writing was never on your horizon before coming to films, how did the script of your first film Ek Main Aur Ek Tu *evolve?*

SB: I got the idea to write my first script after A *Voice in the Sky* was shelved. Something inside me was telling me I must write a story, even though I did not want to direct at that moment. I felt I should have something to show a producer or an actor, and say, 'This is what I want to make.' I did not think of myself as a writer but I had to write a script to tell a story. That is when I met Ayesha DeVitre, Imran's hair stylist, and we began discussing story ideas, exchanging thoughts and writing them down.

I told Imran the idea of the story and he said, '[. . .] why don't you start writing it as a script?' So, Ayesha and I began writing it. It took us a year and a half before Imran was satisfied with the draft. In that period, he was busy with other films but he continued to read our drafts and give feedback. After having spent so much time with the script, I too felt more confident about directing it.

How did you get your first producer, Dharma Productions, to sign with you?

SB: Imran was doing *I Hate Luv Storys* (2010) with Dharma Productions and told me, 'I'm meeting Karan tomorrow. Is it okay if I show your script to him?' I replied, 'Great! Why not?'

Karan was directing *My Name Is Khan* (2010) at that time, but, to my surprise, he called me within a week of Imran giving him my script and said, 'I read your script and I find it interesting. Why don't you come over and meet me?' I was bowled over. I had sent my script to a few other producers over the last six months and one of them was even interested in producing it, but that did not happen.

However, when I met Karan, I was confident he was the one. I felt he cared for the film and thought it was worth making. He gave me pointers and suggestions on the script and said, 'This is what I am thinking. Go back and play with these thoughts, think about what you want to do with them.' Karan never forced or pressured me to accept anything that he suggested. I felt that if he made the film I was going to be the happiest person because he would give me the space to make my own creative decisions! And I was proved right.

What was your first day of shoot like?

SB: On the first day, I was not nervous. On the second day, I was not nervous. On the third day, I was terrified and feeling horrible. On the first day, I ran short of one shot that I thought I would make up for on the next day. On the second day, I ran short of a scene, and on the third day, when I started I was already feeling like I was going to run short of something that day too. I finished the scene on the third day and I did not get all the shots I wanted.

I am reminded of what David Fincher, the director of *Fight Club* (1999), had once said, 'You are not a director unless you have an hour to go and five shots left and you can only take two. When you can make that decision, you are a director.' I look back and realize, you make a wish list of shots you want but on the shoot day you may just have to figure out how to make it work without some of those. That is something I learnt the hard way.

I was reading Martin Scorsese's interview recently and he was talking about the problems he faces in film-making, and I wondered, if *the* Martin Scorsese faces problems, who wouldn't! You just have to understand and accept that a big part of your job is to solve problems that will crop up out of nowhere. You should be open to finding solutions all the time.

Did you ever lose faith in yourself in those six years between film school and your first film?

SB: I chronically suffer from self-doubt. I am a pessimist. I have to drag myself out of these negative moods where something in me tells me if I do not work harder, I will either be out of the industry or dead. I'm usually constantly working hard just to stay afloat. At all times, I fear I am going to drown.

The worst was on day three or four of shooting. We were shooting abroad in winter and lost light by 3 p.m. I was running against time on all three days. Also, it was so cold I had to make an effort to make sure my brain did not freeze, so I could pay attention to the tasks at hand. First, I was shooting Kareena and Imran's gum scene outside the supermarket, then the scene where Imran drops Kareena home after they go to a cafe and Kareena spits on the window. I thought the shot was terrible. I returned to the hotel, upset, thinking what I had shot was shit and I had greatly overestimated my capabilities as a director. I was the wrong person to direct the movie, I was killing my own child and this was going to be a disaster.

I called my writer, Ayesha, to my room, and told her I was going to call Karan to tell him I couldn't direct this movie and that I've made a mistake. Ayesha told me to sleep it off and wait for three or four days to see if I still felt the same. In the next three days, things got better and my confidence returned.

What is an actor possibly looking for in a new director?

SB: An actor is looking for a good script, to begin with. A character that excites them, that they think will be worth putting their effort and time in. They judge if you are the right person to direct that script by judging your understanding of the script and the characters. One is a good script, of course, and second is how a director looks at that script. Moviemaking is a long process and doing it with someone you don't like creates a lot of unnecessary tension. Even you need to like the actors and technicians you choose to work with. If you are cocky, putting everyone down, a know-it-all, don't-question-me-do-as-I-say, no one will want to spend time with you. They need you to be a guy they can easily converse with and make a movie with.

Would learning acting or learning the basics of acting, help a director?

SB: A lot! You will understand what an actor goes through, what their thought process is. Just like any other technician, actors, too, have tools they rely on. Sometimes it is memory, sometimes it is smell. You familiarize yourself with their tools if you know their craft, and this helps you help them use their tools if they need to. For example, if you know about lenses, you can tell your cinematographer exactly what you need, you can be specific and say you want to see the shot through an 85 mm lens. Similarly, if you are a director who has also acted, you can tell your actor what you need is something between anger and rage and even show them how to get to that point. Even if you do not know acting, and you have carefully chosen a sincere cast, they take the character and make it their own and you don't need to do anything but step back and observe them as they give you more than you had imagined.

What are some of the tools a director can use to extract better performances from an actor?

SB: Having said that learning acting will help a director, I do not think it's as much as about learning how to act as it is about giving actors their own space. I am not very experienced as a director but a major part of directing, I think, is knowing when to not 'direct'. Most people think, 'Oh! I am the director so I am supposed to tell them everything all the time.' Interfere or interject only when you think something is wrong. If you think they can get better, tell them how you want them to go about it.

You must have a thorough understanding of your characters. If you know what you are trying to say and the actors are not saying the same thing, it helps to discuss the motivation and the objective of the characters with them.

What do you look for in the audition of an actor?

SB: I am looking for their take on it. It excites me if they do something beyond what I have thought. That's when I cast that actor. I do want them to play it the way I want but I also welcome them to play it the way they want to, and if they do both well, I know I have a winner at hand.

What is a producer looking for in a new director?

SB: A producer probably looks for the same things that an actor does: a good script and the director's point of view on it. For a producer it is important that they trust you with the money they're investing in your script. They need to feel assured that it will be well-spent and the movie will be shot within the scheduled days.

Who was your cinematographer/DOP? Did you block the scenes together?

SB: David McDonald was my DOP on *Ek Main Aur Ek Tu*. He is sixty-nine years young and from Brussels. He has worked for over forty years. Before I began looking for a DOP, I had made a list of the things I liked in some TVCs. He was not my first choice but he was on my wish list.

There were some TV commercials that I really liked, so called their directors to find out who had shot them. Turns out, three of them were shot by David. I wanted to work with him. We also got along well from our first meeting and I just knew he was the right man to work with.

A typical day of shooting would begin with my DOP and me travelling in the same vehicle, so we could talk about the scenes and proposed shots en route. Actors needed time for costume and make-up. Before they came on set, I used to be there with my DOP, having done my shot breakdown. I arrived with a shot list, what I call a schematic, which is a floor plan of the scene with stick figure drawings and camera marks. I talked him through the rough blocking, explaining what was happening in the scene.

Usually during blocking, my assistant directors stood as replacements for the actors so we could visualize their placements and movement. I generally used a viewfinder to decide where I wanted the camera to be placed. We both looked through the viewfinder for possible shots. Once the actors came in, I'd walk them through what I'd decided and ask them if they had any suggestions. A very crucial part of this process for me was to find the key image of the scene. That helped us decide the camera placements and the lighting set-ups.

Some important scenes needed a key image that would define the scene visually. For example, the shot where Imran rubs out his future work schedule and stands gazing at it aimlessly was one. That scene was about making him feel purposeless and lonely. Key images, for me, are the best way to show feelings within a frame.

How do you treat sound in your films?

SB: As a director, I have become more and more aware of how sound is a tool that helps you make your story a lot more believable and impactful. Even if your actors give you their best performance, if the environment around them does not sound correct, there is going to be a sense of it not being 100 per cent real.

There is a sound from my childhood I wish to use someday in my film. We used to stay right next to an Arya Samaj mandir. Both my grandparents and my mother are religious. Back then, they would light a 'havan' every day and go for satsang thrice a week; I would sometimes accompany them. In a satsang, people do not care how they sound while singing, and in the satsangs I went to, I could hear the crackle of fire in between the singing and the hushed whispers of some women in the background. I'd love to use that backdrop someday.

In an industry where a first break is elusive, how important is it to say no, when anyone else in your situation would have said yes?

SB: It is very important and yet tough to say 'no' to something that will really tempt you to say 'yes!' I think the most important no was the one I told my father, before I came to Mumbai, when he persisted and later even tempted me with a car to join him in his business. I guess that was the most important no I ever uttered, and one that paid off very well.

Is ego management one of the skills a director requires?

SB: Big time! Just the idea of being able to work with a variety of talented people towards one common goal requires skill. But I don't think ego is necessarily a bad thing. Any job, anywhere in the world, would demand that you know how to work together with talented and experienced people. We are also in a business where we work with creative people, some of whom have *big* egos. It is a fine balance between respecting them and being able to tell them when you think they are not doing right, without hurting their egos or their feelings. Especially when you are making your first movie, it's very difficult to tell these experienced high achievers that you think what they are giving you is not good enough, but in a way that it doesn't hurt their ego.

What, in the nature of direction, can make a director's job physically and mentally exhausting?

SB: On the one hand, you try to be alone, so you can keep thinking and focusing on matters at hand. On the other hand, you have to communicate clearly with fifty or more people to tell them exactly what you are thinking, so that they can get you what you want. You want to be alone, but you cannot because you need these people and they need you. It is, after all, a collaborative process. The perfect portrayal of the state of a director is in Federico Fellini's 8 ½ (1963). The director is constantly trying to run away from everyone but has nowhere to go. He is stuck with his crew as he is the only one who can tell them what he is thinking, and how he needs things to be done. That is the challenge that makes this profession so stressful, yet fun.

I face situations where I do not want to talk to anybody and someone will come up and ask me a legitimate question, After

I reply, there are more follow-up questions. It is like, you are constantly handling traffic that you want to get out of, but if you get out of it, you will find yourself stuck in a worse jam!

Things do not go according to plan always, because there are so many variables in film-making and the director's job is to let those variables play their part in the evolution of the film, because it is in the unexpected that the magic lies.

Do you enjoy the editing stage?

SB: Yes. Editing is the time you see your vision—the movie— come together bit by bit.

When I saw the first cut, I thought there were a lot of things that were not working and could be fixed. I did feel that there were a few things we couldn't fix, but in the end, we did. To be honest, there was this one time when I saw it and I thought it was shit and would not come together. Then I felt it was the first half that was not working so we worked on the edit and it looked better. After we edited the first half, I was satisfied and moved on to the second. When we started editing the second half, I thought even that was not working! Then we worked on it and made it look better. Once I was satisfied, I viewed both the halves and decided that the first was not working! It drove me crazy.

At that time what role did your editor play?

SB: My editor boosted my confidence by assuring me that the edit was working. Sometimes you are so close to what you want that you lose objectivity. Editors really help a director with developing a perspective. I think sometimes they change the pace of the scene and sometimes they change how the scene was written. That is the making of a good editor . . . when they can make a scene that was not working earlier, work. They can change the pace of how a scene flows from one to the other.

When you make your subsequent films, is there any particular feeling you would like to keep alive from your first film-making experience?

SB: I would like to keep the element of nervousness alive because it makes you take that little extra step; it keeps you on your toes. I don't want to get too confident and too sure about myself. I was lucky to get a foot in the door and now I have to barge in and make a place for myself!

Is film-making for you a destination or a journey?

SB: For me, it is a journey. I want to keep making movies for as long as I can keep finding things that interest and excite me. I do not want to make three movies and stop because that would mean I have been seeking them as a destination. I hope I am talented enough to keep myself afloat on this journey. I would say that even if I were not directing independently right now, I would still be working in the film industry. I enjoyed and will continue to enjoy the process of making films regardless of being or not being a director.

In what way do you think you have evolved as a director from your very first experience?

SB: I think I have evolved overall as a person and as a storyteller. I hope the small things I learnt, such as how a performance starts to work while shooting, how to block a scene better, among others, will help me make my next movie better. I have definitely evolved and it is difficult to put a percentage to it. When you do something continuously, you get a hang of it and get better at it, so I hope to make another film and continue to strive to be better.

Is there anything you would like to share with others today, something that can help them in anyway?

SB: I would tell everyone to stick to what they love. It is as simple as that. It is a very clichéd thing to say, but stick to what you love and what you want to do with your time and life. If you leave, perhaps you did not love it in the first place. The idea is to know what you love, and once you know that, I believe, you will not leave it for anybody or anything. You will keep at it, come what may.

SHYAM BENEGAL

'When I was shooting my first feature film, Ankur, I had to travel to a location over 30 km away from our hotel every day. Along the way, we would pass by a centre that housed a tank regiment. Their motto was "Bash on Regardless". That gave me a great deal of confidence and continues to when I have a particularly difficult challenge to overcome.'

FILMOGRAPHY

Ankur (1974); *Charandas Chor* (1975); *Nishant* (1975); *Manthan* (1976); *Bhumika* (1977); *Kondura* (1978); *Junoon* (1978); *Anugraham* (1978); *Kalyug* (1981); *Arohan* (1982); *Mandi* (1983); *Trikal* (1985); *Susman* (1987); *Antarnaad* (1991); *Suraj Ka Satvan Ghoda* (1992); *Mammo* (1994); *Sardari Begum* (1996); *The Making of the Mahatma* (1996); *Samar* (1999); *Hari-Bhari* (2000); *Zubeidaa* (2001); *Netaji Subhas Chandra Bose: The Forgotten Hero* (2005); *Welcome to Sajjanpur* (2008); *Well Done Abba* (2010)

SNEAK PEEK

Shyam Benegal was born and brought up in Hyderabad. After getting his master's in economics, he arrived in Bombay for his first job with National Advertising Service in 1958. In 1959, he joined Lintas and directed his first commercial for a product called Hima Peas. He used to make around 150 commercials a year with Lintas. He directed his first documentary *Gher Betha Ganga* in 1962, which was about the Mahi river project in Gujarat. He taught a short course on film-making at FTII, Pune, in 1966. He made over 900 commercial shorts, including documentaries, before he directed *Ankur* in 1973. Since his first job in advertising to his first feature film as director, it had been a journey of fifteen years.

MY TAKE

I met Shyam Benegal for this interview several times over four years, as he was occupied with writing a television miniseries on the making of the Indian Constitution, titled *Samvidhan*, and a ninety-minute-long history of Punjab, *Jung-e-Azadi*.

On my first visit to his office, I felt quite comfortable. His desk was surrounded by tall bookshelves containing titles in a variety of languages on a variety of subjects. The window shades were drawn. Lots of light, as befits a place of higher learning.

During our sessions, I discovered that he was very patient. His interest in my book was tangible. He was affectionate and always addressed me by my first name. He always apologized profusely whenever he'd have to cancel any of our meetings. When I would meet him, he would apologize for making me come all the way to his office and later insist that I have tea with him.

Once, when I had called him for an appointment, he read out a newspaper article over the phone that mentioned that my ancestors were from Iraq. He told me he had thought of me when he read the article and wanted me to read it too. I had never met him prior to my writing this book, and yet, he was warm and welcoming every time we met.

His 'dissatisfaction' fascinates me. I say dissatisfaction because despite his long and wonderful career he keeps chasing the high of completing a project as though film-making is as essential to him as breathing.

THE CONVERSATION

Rakesh Bakshi: *Thank you for being a part of this book. Where were you born? What was it in your childhood that drew you towards cinema?*

Shyam Benegal (SB): I was born in a town called Trimulgherry [Tirumalagiri], a British army cantonment town near Hyderabad. The first ten years of my life were spent there. There was a cinema hall that belonged to the army garrison; it was called Garrison Cinema. There were three changes of programme each week: a south Indian film, a Hindi film and an English film on the weekends. I preferred the English films, because I found them more credible than the others.

In fact, after my very first film as a viewer, I made up my mind that I wanted to be a film-maker for the simple reason that no other form of art or entertainment offered an experience quite like cinema. It took you to a completely different world. Not like a dream, but a world that one could see, hear and respond to; a world *almost* as real as our own. This was the kind of world I wanted to create.

Being a photographer, my father portrayed images of people and the world around him. But they were still photographs. I was not interested in that. I was interested in creating moving pictures. He had a hand-cranked movie projector, which could show films in three different gauges: 35mm, 16mm and 9.5mm. He also had a 16-mm movie camera with which he made films that often featured his many children. These films were shown to guests who were invited for dinner, as post-dinner entertainment. I spent a lot of time in my father's photography studio because I could sit and draw there while he was working in the dark room.

One advantage of living in the cantonment was that you met people from different parts of the country. You learnt how to be secular, inclusive and free of chauvinistic prejudices. My father was a great believer in education for both men and women. He saw to it that all his children went to school and college, particularly his daughters.

A traumatic experience of my childhood was when my parent's home was publicly auctioned while we were still living in it. I must have been eleven and I was shattered.

As a child or during your youth, were you an avid reader?

SB: I was lucky in many ways. I had an uncle, Benegal Dinkar Rao. He had walked all the way from Rangoon to Calcutta during the Japanese invasion of Burma. He introduced me to literature, both Indian and European. Stories by Premchand and Rabindranath Tagore, the Ramayana, the Mahabharata and other Puranic stories. I was also introduced to different writers of fiction, such as Daphne Du Maurier, Ernest Hemingway, Charles Dickens and Charles and Mary Lamb's adaptations of Shakespeare's plays.

His greatest gift to me was to make me curious about life, about the world around us. He loved to look at the stars and seek out constellations—Orion, Sagittarius, Gemini—and ask me their names. He opened up the world beyond my own home, the little world situated in the immensity of the universe.

One afternoon, he took my brother and me to watch a film. On the way home, we stopped by a bar where he wanted to have a glass of beer. He asked us whether we would like to have some. I shook my head vigorously and said no. He then told me that before I say yes or no to anything, I have to find out what it is. He made us taste the beer. I hated it but at least I now knew what it tasted like. I mention all these things because these were significant influences beyond how the home and school environments influenced me.

Did you grow up learning music or the arts?

SB: I am tone deaf [*laughs*]! However, I was introduced to Western classical music by a gentleman whose surname was Engineer.

In fact, he ran a workshop that serviced cars and jeeps. He was a Western-classical-music buff and had a huge collection of 78-rpm vinyl records. A childhood friend, Jaswant, had spoken to me about Mr Engineer and his collection of music. What is more, Mr Engineer was actually an employee of Jaswant's uncle. When I met him and expressed my desire to listen to his collection of music, he asked me to come to his house. I told him I had about forty-five minutes after lunch before I went back to class.

He decided to get me to listen to his collection in a chronological order of composers, starting with medieval European to classical and romantic composers of the nineteenth century. He would patiently explain the specific characteristics of the different composers, Italian, German and Russian.

At about the same time, I had some excellent professors in my college. They introduced me to thinkers and writers like Jean-Paul Sartre, Karl Marx, Leo Tolstoy, Alexander Pushkin and Fyodor Dostoyevsky. My time at Nizam College was an extremely stimulating one. I edited the college magazine for a couple of years and was the president of the English union for a year. Osmania University had, at that time, acquired an entire collection of literature from the Americas, France, Germany and Russia for its library. I read books by Rainer Maria Rilke, Thomas Mann, Ernest Hemingway and John Steinbeck among others. I also directed plays in English, one of which was T.S. Eliot's *Murder in the Cathedral*.

Your first film dealt with caste prejudice, social hierarchy, adultery and gender in a patriarchal society. Was it inspired by real incidents?

SB: During my early years of college, I had this friend who helped look after his father's farm not far from where we lived. He had an affair with one of the women working on the farm who belonged to a caste lower than his and whom he soon abandoned. I wrote a short story based on this event for my college magazine. Later, I worked on it and converted it into a film script, which became the basis of my first feature film many years later. The version of the script from which I made the film came after scores of drafts written over a decade.

The first couple of decades after India's independence was a time of change for the Indian countryside. The feudal structure was crumbling and new land reforms were being introduced in some of the states.

Do you have a memory of the first film you saw?

SB: My first memory of a film I saw in a cinema hall was a Hollywood film, *Cat People* (1942). It was a horror film. I was fascinated and terrified, at the same time! Films create an alternative world that you enter during the duration of the film. This is what fascinated me and continues to fascinate me today.

My elder brother and I befriended the projectionist at Garrison Cinema. He allowed us to watch films from the projection booth, saving us the cost of buying tickets. In any case, our parents never gave us money to see more than one film a month. Thanks to the projectionist at Garrison Cinema, I could watch ten to twelve films a month. Soon I discovered and became a fan of directors William Wyler, Billy Wilder and John Huston, apart from film stars Tyrone Power, Errol Flynn and John Wayne.

The projectionist allowed my brother and me to take film cuttings that littered the floor of the booth. We would splice these film cuttings together and view them at home on our father's magic lantern.

Did you have a dream in childhood?

SB: Yes, a single dream, to become a film-maker! Later, during my years in college, I read a great deal on and about cinema and films. It was when I saw Satyajit Ray's *Pather Panchali* (1955) that I found the path and direction I would take to make my own kind of films and not try to imitate anyone else.

My father believed one should never give up on what one really wants to do simply because the goal is difficult or appears impossible. But I was living in a place where there was no film industry. The closest places where films were made were Madras [Chennai], Bombay [Mumbai] and Calcutta [Kolkata]. There was neither any chance nor opportunity for me to travel to these far-off places to either learn film-making or work with film-makers. If I had told my father at that time that I wanted to be a film-maker, he would have thought I had a hole in my head. Therefore, I studied economics for my bachelor's as well as master's degrees.

When did you arrive in this profession, or Mumbai?

SB: I came to Mumbai looking for film-related work in 1958. I lived with the director, Guru Dutt, for a month and later, with his mother for a year. He asked me to join him as an assistant. I did not want to, because that way I would be just one of the several assistants and gofers (go-for) under him.

Moreover, I really did not want to make the kind of films he made, even though he was someone I held in high regard and he inspired me. Later, I took my script (*Ankur*) to various producers. No one agreed to make it. I was told that no one would be interested in seeing a film about an upper-caste landlord sleeping with his Dalit domestic help. The script did the rounds for the next thirteen years till I finally found a willing producer!

What did you do professionally for those thirteen years? Did you seek a job as an assistant director?

SB: I did not seek a job as an assistant director because I felt I would get too influenced by the director and end up making the kind of films they were making. The existing popular form of cinema of the time was not my cup of tea. It did not allow me to express myself, or to be connected to the social environment of which I was a part. It was not integral to my reality.

So, what was the plan of action then?

SB: It was not hard for me to figure out that I could be a film-maker. I wrote reasonably well. Throughout my school and college years I was always engaged in writing and it was often appreciated. Therefore, I knew it was not too difficult for me to become a copywriter with an advertising agency. It was an environment where I could interact with film producers and directors of advertising films in my normal course of work. Soon, I was writing and directing advertising films myself while hoping that I would find a producer for my own feature film.

How did you proceed in your career after becoming a copywriter?

SB: I began as a copywriter with National Advertising Service in 1958 and joined Lintas soon after. Lintas was a far more congenial place for me to work. Within six months, my boss, Alyque Padamsee, knowing my interest in films suggested that I try my hand at directing advertising films.

Advertising films was a new profession at that time, this was in 1959–60. It had started only a decade ago. I began writing and directing advertising films. My first advertisement film was for Hindustan Lever's dehydrated green peas, Hima Peas. There was no TV those days, so advertising films would play at cinema halls across the country. Gradually, I began to participate in all areas of film-making. Within a couple of years, I was making an average of hundred advertising films a year. I became so busy that I hardly had any time left to do anything else other than sleep at night.

What path did you choose to learn direction?

SB: I was never an assistant to any director. I began as a director. There were experienced film-makers, both documentary and fiction, who used to produce advertising films, such as Clement Baptista, V.M. Vijaykar and Durga Khote and Fali Bilimoria.

Therefore, I never felt any kind of anxiety about my own ability to direct, even though I had to learn from scratch and all by myself.

I am not sure whether it was easier to direct since the script was also written by me. I am not sure whether doing it my way was better than going through a film school prior to becoming a director. Perhaps, it would have made the learning process quicker and easier had I studied at a film school. FTII started much later in 1961. At one time, I used to regret not having been formally educated in cinema. I would have learned more systematically than the way I was compelled to.

Learning on your own means that you have to learn everything from the very beginning. If you come via a film school you don't need to reinvent the wheel.

How did you find a producer for Ankur?

SB: Mohan Bijlani and Freni Variava were my first producers. They were partners in a company called Blaze Advertising Services, which was the largest distributor of advertising films in India prior to the introduction of national TV, which then offered TV channels for advertising commercials and spots.

Blaze had a number of theatres under them, about 3500 of the 6500 that existed at the time. They supplied these theatres with advertising films week after week. Lintas made the largest number of advertising films and Blaze was the primary distributor for them. While working for Lintas I got to know Mohan Bijlani quite well. He knew that I had been pitching my film script to various producers for several years.

Finally, at a social gathering, Mohan Bijlani good humouredly taunted me, 'You keep telling everybody that you want to make films but why aren't you actually making one?' I retorted, 'You give me the money and I will make one right now.' To which he replied, 'I will give you the money only if the film does not cost too much.' I told him I only needed 5.5 lakhs, to which he immediately agreed. I thanked him and said I would take a rain check on his generous offer since I had accepted a fellowship that would keep me busy for at least a year, during which I would be abroad for several months. Once I returned, I was ready to make the film.

How did you get your actors onboard?

SB: Casting is always a challenge. I had Waheeda Rehman in mind to play the protagonist. She had done some fine work with Guru Dutt and Vijay Anand. I was acquainted with her as she had worked with Guru Dutt. However, she appeared somewhat reluctant. I discovered she had had an unfortunate experience with regional-language films and was not sure that doing my film was the right choice at a time when she was one of the most sought-after stars of the film industry. And I felt she was not particularly confident in my ability as a director.

Soon after, I approached a south Indian actress, Sharda, who had recently won a National Award for one of her performances. She readily agreed and readily changed her mind. Several female stars refused to act in my film; the reason being that the character I had in mind sleeps with a man other than her husband and after getting pregnant, insists on keeping the child. Even potential producers had a problem with a central female character (heroine) of this kind.

Among the several actresses I approached were Aparna Sen and Anju Mahendu. Anju had modelled for me earlier in several commercials, and I found her to be an extremely capable actress. But I was not quite sure that she would be right for the part since she had a very strong urban-middle-class personality, while my character belonged to the rural lower class.

My chief assistant at that time mentioned a person he knew who happened to have been in college with him. This was Shabana Azmi. He mentioned that she was from a film family and had done theatre in St Xavier's College and was extremely talented. On meeting her, I was absolutely certain that she was the one I was looking for. What is more, Shabana could also speak the Hyderabadi dialect, as her mother was from Hyderabad and she had several cousins living there. Her performance in the film turned out to be outstanding. In many ways, she owned the film. She won her first National Award, among several others, in 1973 for *Ankur*.

I had cast a young man called Ajay Goel in the role of the landlord's son. His father was a well-known film producer. However, a week before the unit was to travel to the location, which was near Hyderabad, Ajay came down with jaundice. I was stuck. I had no actor to play this crucial part. I turned to my friend, Satyadev Dubey, who had also written the dialogues, for help in casting. He came up with the name of a young man, Anant Nag. I did not feel the need to hold an audition for him. *Ankur* was not only Anant's first film but also the one that helped him embark on a hugely successful career as a star in Kannada cinema.

How do you normally cast actors? What are you looking for in actors when you hold auditions for them?

SB: I have never held any auditions for any of my films. As and when I did, those films never got made! [*Laughs.*] The only actor whom I have ever held an audition for was Kulbhushan Kharbanda, for my second film, *Nishant*. He came all the way from Calcutta to Bombay for the audition. His audition was simply a formality. I took him directly to Hyderabad the next day for the shoot. He had come to the audition without any real hope of getting a part in the film. Therefore, he had parked his car at the Calcutta airport to travel back home on his return the next day. I presume that his car remained at Calcutta airport for a long time until it was finally towed away by the municipal authorities.

I generally judge actors on the basis of the personality they project, and whether they can assume the personality that I need to create for the film. I usually observe their body language and also whether they are photogenic, by this I mean, whether they are capable of projecting a distinct personality that could be captured by the camera.

I also look for commitment in an actor. Take someone like Naseeruddin Shah. He is a highly committed actor and always gives his very best to whatever he does. Commitment is as important as talent. Commitment to their craft and instinct are primary requirements in an actor. Smita Patil, for instance, was very instinctive. She had no formal training as an actor. She developed her craft as she went on.

Did you do any kind of script workshops with actors?

SB: No. It was only later, when I made a major TV series, *Bharat Ek Khoj*, where I needed a very large number of actors, that I needed to hold workshops in order to save production time.

Actors do not need to know anything versus actors need to know everything, what do you employ when directing actors?

SB: For me, the important thing is, they must understand the character they are playing. I begin by telling them the story in detail, so that they know what is motivating their characters at any given time. To get a convincing performance, actors should be convinced of what they are doing. I spend a lot of time before the shoot, speaking to my actors about their characters and the story of the film. This helps in bringing out the complexities of their characters. I also organize workshops when actors need specific skills to play their characters. In *Bhumika*, Smita played a well-known Marathi actress of the 1930s whose range of performance extended from action films to domestic dramas. Smita had to learn horse-riding, fencing and dancing for *Bhumika*. I arranged for her to attend these classes every morning. Om Puri learnt to weave cloth at a weaver's village to prepare for his role in *Susman*.

You made documentaries before making your first feature. What special skills did those experiences give you that helped you evolve as a film director?

SB: Making documentaries helped me seek real locations for shooting my feature films. Making advertising films taught me how to get the maximum from every visual and sound in each given image. For example, if you write an impactful story in 3000 words, in advertising you have to get the same impact using no more than 200 words. You have to be precise in your expression and concise in your word use.

TV and cinema are two different things. A cinematic feature is equivalent to a novel. A TV feature is more like a story for a magazine. Advertising is persuasive communication to help sell a product or service. Its value as entertainment is not an end in itself.

There is a lot of difference between documentary and fiction films; documentaries deal with facts and are an unobtrusive way of recording facts, documenting whatever is happening on the basis of the subject you have chosen. The documentary-maker functions as an observer; they sometimes also intervene by interpreting and offering comments and views—a view that may emerge from what you have shot or you may have a view on the basis of which you made the film as an illustration.

As a fiction film-maker, the experience of making documentaries is very useful. It sensitizes you to moments that are not repeatable. Sometimes, when you are shooting a documentary, you may have something in your peripheral vision that would add value to what you are doing within the frame. You may notice things happening beyond the frame, beyond what you scripted and blocked. Things from the world outside of the area within which you are working is something you can take advantage of while making a documentary. Your power of observation and your ability to notice things around you become sharper; you are far more aware of your environment. If you take everything for granted, you don't notice anything, you observe nothing and you learn nothing.

What kind of self-confidence and courage do you need to be a film-maker, which you experienced while making your first feature or subsequent ones?

SB: It has to do with confidence and the chances you are willing to take, rather than courage, that you can see things through even if you do not know how.

A few years ago, I was shooting in Haryana in the month of March. It is a time of the year when there is hardly any cloud or rain. I was picturizing a song, I had fire engines loaded and ready with water to create rain. The area had several peacocks and peahens. I was hoping to see the peacocks preening in the rain. Peacocks, as we found out soon, however, do not preen unless it rains naturally. On the second day of the shoot, dark clouds suddenly appeared and there was a cloudburst! It did not rain long, but it was enough for the peacocks in the area to preen. We were lucky enough to capture the event.

What is the difference between writing a novel and a film script? What makes for a good writer–director relationship?

SB: There is a difference between a novelist and a film scriptwriter. A writer who writes novels only uses his imagination. A film director wants the scriptwriter to customize his or her writing according to the director's vision and requirement. That is the fundamental difference.

The writer and director relationship can work only when both of them understand each other well. If somebody gives me a script and asks me to make a film based on it, and if the script does not inspire me in any way or does not suit my sensibility, the film I will make from such a script will be mediocre at best. I believe, the director has to be the author of the film, only then will they be able to harness and give direction to the creative contribution of the others involved in the process. There will always be some difference in sensibilities between two individuals. Although, there can be shared sensibilities. For instance, the sensibility that writer Abrar Alvi shared with his director Guru Dutt. They had a fine relationship. The way the characters were etched in Guru Dutt's films matched both their sensibilities. This is very important. You don't often see examples of that kind. I have had an excellent working relationship with eminent writers such as Girish Karnad, Shama Zaidi and Atul Tiwari, apart from late Satyadev Dubey.

What was your process of blocking a scene?

SB: Govind Nihalani, my cinematographer, and I developed an understanding that helped a great deal. When I was making *Ankur*, the script was quite sketchy and I allowed the actors to improvise and fill in the blanks. The way the actors physically related to each other often determined the camera placement.

I usually block the scene after breaking it down in terms of the different shots that need to be taken that would collectively constitute the scene. I work out the overall space in which the scene is to take place to block the scene initially. Then, I let the actors into the space for a camera rehearsal. Sometimes we change the camera angle a little depending on factors like the actor's movements, the lighting pattern or the plan for the sequence.

As a director, you do not force or impose anything. What you decide for the actors or the camera has to fit into your scheme of things but your scheme is not inflexible; however, its flexibility is limited by the way you want to tell your story. The narrative style does not necessarily change. You may shape the scenes a little depending on the ability of the actors, the vantage points of the camera, the kind of lenses you can use in that situation and the overall lighting plan. All of these have to be factored in.

Why are cinematographers and directors considered best friends on set?

SB: They say that the cinematographer is the director's eyes, the sound engineer constitutes his ears and the actors are the interpreters.

A director should not impose a visual design at the cost of the narrative, or at the cost of storytelling. Neither should a cinematographer. Once you take that route, you are caught up in technique and the substance and its essence are lost.

I was told that when you go to shoot a film in any location, you take your main crew and actors to the location of the shoot to mingle with the locals. Why?

SB: I did do that in the past, when all of us had the luxury of time. It was also not as expensive to do as it is today. However, I still think it is an excellent opportunity because it helps everyone get familiar with the world that is going to be recreated in the film. Today, this may be seen as a needless indulgence that is unnecessarily expensive. Nowadays, you rarely have the actors with you through the entire schedule as it is unaffordable.

When I was shooting *Nishant* and *Ankur*, my actors were with me from the first day of the shoot to the last, even those who were not required for most of the days. For instance, Kulbhushan Kharbanda, who played an important part in *Nishant*, used to get into his costume and make-up and be on the sets every day even though I shot with him only on the last six days of a forty-five-day schedule. By the time I filmed with him, there was no question of my directing him. He was already steeped in that world and knew his part very well.

During *Ankur*, I made Shabana eat her meals seated on the floor, just like the character [Lakshmi] she played. All the others ate their meals at the table. During *Manthan*, I made the actors wear their character-costumes, which were stitched in the village, all through the period of the film's shooting, so that their clothes looked properly worn. In *Bhumika*, which was set between 1930 and 1950, I got the actors to wear costumes from Guru Dutt's *Kaagaz Ke Phool* (1959). The music composer Vanraj [Bhatia] used the music style of that period.

Who was the editor of your first film and what is your normal process of working with an editor?

SB: Bhanudas Divkar was my editor since the time I started making advertising films in 1960s. He edited my advertising films, including documentaries. He edited all my films until he passed away.

My normal practice is to work with my editor as soon as they have assembled the footage according to the scenes. I sit with them to work out the pace and tenor of the film in terms of its emotional content. Often, the editor will surprise you with a certain cut or suggestion. Aseem Sinha, my editor, is also one of those who surprise you with their sixth sense. He has been my editor for a very long time, almost nineteen years.

I pay a lot of attention to the colour and texture of the image. The emotional quality of an image is also very important to me, because it breathes life into the characters. It is akin to the moment when the fragrance of a dish almost cooked permeates the air, alerting you to the quality of the food. An editor has a large part to play in making that happen.

Do you prefer to shoot the most challenging scenes or the easy ones on the very first day?

SB: My first day of shooting can start any which way, from any part of the narrative—a simple, difficult or complicated scene does not make any difference to me. In the case of *Ankur*, we shot sequentially since it was possible for us to shoot it that way. The entire film was required to be shot in a single location for the most part. One of the reasons I chose to do that was because my actors were all new and it was easier to take them through the narrative of the story in a linear and sequential way, which would help them in pitching their performance. Luckily, it was possible to do due to the single location and the nature of the location.

Some first-time directors get overwhelmed by the inevitable questions from the technicians on shoot or the ones in their own heads, such as, 'Where to place the camera?'

SB: Camera placement depends on how you wish to tell the story and the kind of story you are narrating. It does not pose any kind of challenge in such situations.

At the beginning of your feature film career, in spite of all the experience you had making commercials and documentaries, did you feel there were some shortcomings that you overcame during the process of making subsequent films?

SB: Yes, I felt I had some shortcoming in every department! When you start making a film, even if you have made many films, it is always the first day of your first film, it does not matter how many you may have made before. If you asked great musicians like Pandit Ravi Shankar or Hari Prasad Chaurasia how they managed to make great music sound original each time, I am certain even they would say, 'I do not know how it happens!'

Some first-time film-makers panic when they watch their first rushes, dailies, etc. What has been your experience personally and what is your advice to any first-time film-maker?

SB: What worried me the most was when I saw the first cut of my first film. I seemed to lack control over the length of the scenes and I had not yet developed any real judgement on the pace of a scene. Pace is very important. To tell your story well you have to pace it correctly. If a scene lingers longer than it should or tends to rush through, it will not register with the viewer and making such a call depends solely on your ability to judge whether it is working well or not. If you are telling a story that interests the audience, they will go along with you, travel at your pace. But learning to achieve this is not easy. You can take the audience hurtling down a route or walk with them at a gentle pace, allowing them to soak in the environment as long as they do not lose the narrative thread.

What are the perks as a first-time film-maker you will always miss when you make your subsequent films?

SB: When you make your first film and it is shown to an audience, you are presenting yourself, flaws and all. When you make a documentary, you do not present and reveal yourself in the same way. In documentaries, you have an axe to grind, you have a purpose that goes beyond the film. The documentary film is a vehicle to present a point of view or an exploration of any subject. The primary job of a feature film is to provide entertainment. First-time film-makers of cinema or documentaries are more adventurous, they do not know the depth of the well when they leap into it. It is a very different experience when you have that knowledge. Fear comes later, with experience.

On the positive side, you learn to cope with it as you move forward with the knowledge you gain from each film you make. First-time film-makers start with a great deal of innocence. If after the first film, you continue to display the same kind of naivety, it is simply ignorance.

If your own child wanted to be a film-maker, what would your advice be?

SB: I would never discourage them. I would just remind them that it is a lot of hard work. You can choose anything to do as long as you are willing to work hard for it. I would caution them against thinking of film-making as an easy way to make a living. It is difficult, laborious and often quite boring. You just have to remember that. You have to go by your inclination and ability. If you have the ability, go for it. If you are doing it because I, your father, am a film-maker, think again. You have to make a conscious choice of your own.

Would you like to say something, share something from your experiences with today's generation?

SB: See, if you choose to do something in life, you cannot harbour ifs and buts. You have to be fully committed. If you have alternatives, check them out before you make a commitment. There is no looking back once you make a commitment.

When I was shooting my first feature film, *Ankur*, I had to travel to a location over 30 km away from our hotel every day. Along the way, we would pass by a centre that housed a tank regiment. Their motto was 'Bash on Regardless'. That gave me a great deal of confidence and continues to when I have a particularly difficult challenge to overcome.

MOHIT SURI

'The best reference you can ever have, better than any film or book or mentor/teacher, is you. Just you!'

FILMOGRAPHY

Zeher (2005); *Kalyug* (2005); *Woh Lamhe* (2006); *Awarapan* (2007); *Raaz: The Mystery Continues* (2009); *Crook* (2010); *Murder 2* (2011); *Aashiqui 2* (2013); *Ek Villain* (2014); *Hamari Adhuri Kahani* (2015); *Half Girlfriend* (2017)

SNEAK PEEK

Mohit was born and brought up in Mumbai and has lived in Chennai, Ahmedabad and Hyderabad. He became an assistant disc jockey (DJ) when he was in the Class XI or XII; his first job in films was as the production runner with Vishesh Films in 1999. His first film as an assistant director was *Kasoor* (2001) with Vikram Bhatt. He directed certain portions of Anurag Basu's *Tumsa Nahin Dekha* (2004), when the latter fell ill. He directed his first film *Zeher* in 2005. Since his first job as production runner with Vishesh Films to his first film as director, also with Vishesh Films, it had been a journey of six years.

MY TAKE

I had always found Mohit's films to be grounded in reality. When I saw his second film, *Kalyug*, I thought, if I were a producer,

I would sign this young director right away. It was only after that I saw *Zeher*.

When I met Mohit for this anthology, he was one of the few people who told me I had a great book ahead of me and that he was humbled at being brought onboard and alongside great directors such as Bhatt Saab. I was encouraged when he, on his own accord, called me up after reading his first draft to tell me he really liked it. I wish he could've seen my big smile upon hearing this.

Once out of the blue, he called me to say that he had met someone who was producing a TV show on the same lines as my book was and he could put us in touch if that would help me in some way. I could never forget that phone call. It went further to reaffirm my belief that he was someone who would volunteer his skill, talent, knowledge, experience and help to someone who could benefit by it. He gave the impression of being an extremely self-reliant person, not only in making films but also on a personal level. I found him to be someone who was open, warm and reflective and had a passionate, raw energy.

In addition, if there was something that was as dear to him as film-making and storytelling, it was this: a life companion, a life partner, a lifelong friend. I saw this desire reflected in his film *Aashiqui 2*.

THE CONVERSATION

Rakesh Bakshi: *Thank you for being a part of our book.*

Mohit Suri (MS): I liked the subject of your book *Directors' Diaries* from the get-go. I remember, you had mentioned that you are a film-maker-turned-author because you chose to do what you love, writing. I have always believed that what you do in life, the choices you make, leave an imprint. Those imprints, someday, help you create your picture, your painting, your book, your song. You mentioned you chose to write a book without knowing if it were the right or wrong thing to do, because until now you have aspired to be a film-maker. One of the primary principles of directing is making choices, you have to make one about whether something is right or wrong, because there is no middle ground. As a director, you make a choice and then stick with it, all the way. Moreover, I would definitely want to read about the lives of the other directors who are a part of this book.

Where were you born and brought up? What do you remember fondly from those years?

MS: I was born in Bombay. Mahesh and Mukesh Bhatt are my maternal uncles. My maternal grandfather, Nanabhai Bhatt, had made around a hundred films. However, he went bankrupt by the end of his life when all his films' negatives got burnt in a fire at Film Centre in Tardeo.

My father worked with a corporate and was posted at various cities. And so, I have lived in Madras, Ahmedabad and Hyderabad. While living in south India, we were isolated because of the linguistic gap and my inability to pick up the local language. Even though I was kind of alone, I was never bored. I would make up stories about my toys that my family later told me were very imaginative.

Emraan [Hashmi] is my cousin; his grandmother, Poornima Verma, was an actress, and had come to Chennai to meet us. She would say about me, this boy is going to become a director, or he will do something in films. But my mother didn't want me to be a part of that industry as my grandfather had gone bankrupt as a film-maker.

When I was five, we returned to Bombay from Madras. That is the first time I met my uncles and was exposed to the film side of my mother's family. I have a hazy memory of spending my summer vacations with Emraan. Bandra was a microcosm of India, with people from different parts and linguistic backgrounds living together. During riots provoked by fundamentalists, people of all faiths got together to patrol the locality so no one from any religion was harmed. My father is a Punjabi and I even some have Christian cousins. That has given me a very secular point of view about every aspect of life and work. I was eight years old and we were living in Bombay when my mother passed away. My sister started living with my grandmother, and my father and I stayed together.

Without your mother's presence, was it hard making crucial decisions? Like, making a career choice?

MS: Without my mother, I didn't have anybody to direct my point of view in life. When you lose a mother—yes, you may still have your father's financial security—you lose out on the tender/protective side that a mother provides. Someone who ensures that you eat your meals on time and wants to feed you even when you are not hungry. I had to look after myself. My father never believed in censorship; he would say, you are a product of how you interpret things, so it does not really matter what you read and watch! My father brought me up like a friend, so he did not mind me watching adult content, not that we sat together to watch adult films. That's maybe why I have never debated whether to depict sexuality in my films or not. If the subject demands sexuality, the film must reflect it.

When I was a teenager, after we saw the pre-release shows of *Aashiqui* (1990), *Dil Hai Ke Maanta Nahin* (1991) and *Sadak* (1991), my uncle, Mukesh-ji, would always ask me my opinion on the films we had seen. On hearing my views, he would tell me, 'You can become a director someday.'

My father never came to school to receive my report card so I was the only child allowed to collect my own report card. I did not allow myself to use my mother's death as an excuse to fail academically. My life was guided by the thought, 'If I do not do things for myself, no one will tell me to do it, nor will anyone do it for me.' That alone gave me the motivation to do whatever

I needed to for a better life. And, I think, I carried that belief to film-making too. That's why I believe that a director has to have his own point of view to make his film.

When was the earliest your instinct told you to do something that must have been very unusual at that time?

MS: I must have been sixteen, in Class XII, when my father decided to remarry. Even though he was like a friend to me, I felt rebellious about his decision to remarry. I wanted to become financially independent so I could be more on my own. I became an assistant music DJ to a friend. I learnt how to remix songs. When I was making my first film, I used these skills to remix an original song 'Woh Lamhe'. Until then, film-makers were only remixing old classics. I remixed a new song and it was a big hit.

Your earliest memory of watching movies?

MS: *Do Aur Do Paanch* (1980) and *Haathi Mere Saathi*, as I am very fond of animals. Hrishikesh Mukherjee is amongst the many directors whose films influenced me greatly. The frame of his films was never beautiful in an unreal way, never larger than life. Therefore, it always felt as though I was watching someone's life unfold when I watched his films. Shots from Mahesh Bhatt's films, *Zakhm* (1998), *Daddy* (1989) and *Arth* (1982) also left an impression on me. I remember thinking these shots were more images of performances than dialogue scenes.

When my mother was very ill, almost on her deathbed, I entered the house all drenched in the rain. She told me to leave my shoes outside. This is how some mundane scene in a film could connect with me, through these small moments. Some images in films resonate with me on a personal level, and when I watch them, I feel, 'Oh, this happened to me too.' I am more interested in an image reflecting my own life rather than a picture that is only a good-looking frame, and with which I can neither connect nor understand. These images stay with me the longest. I have often used images and moments from my own life in my films. I've seen my father and his second wife arguing a lot and I used that in my very first film as director, *Zeher*.

You write your films. Did you write stories as a child?

MS: I began writing stories at seventeen, when I fell in love with a girl from my school. I was attracted to her because she was interested in literature and she wrote well and read interesting novels. Influenced by her, I began reading literature too.

Did you want to be a film-maker since your teenage years?

MS: When I was a teenager, my grandmother used to tell me, 'You are cut out for films,' to which I'd say, 'I am doing well in my studies, I do not want to be in films.' Ever since I was ten, I wanted to travel to space. Even now, when I visit places from where you can see a clear sky, I stargaze for hours.

My job as an assistant DJ was not earning me enough money. I wanted to study aerospace engineering. I managed to secure a seat in a college abroad. However, two days before I was scheduled to leave the country for the admission process, my father informed me he could not support me financially for my education abroad.

I loved my father, but I was determined to move out of his house and live on my own terms. I remembered Mukesh-ji had told me, '[. . .] You are a very smart boy, you should work in the films with me.' Forty-eight hours after my father's declaration, I approached my aunt, Kumkum Sehgal, who worked with Mukesh-ji. I told her I wanted a job because I wanted to make my own money. She immediately took me to his office and I told him I would like to take him up on his job offer. I was still in Class XII then. I joined him the next day. Honestly, it was my way to rebel against my father. In hindsight I can say that sometimes hate can motivate you more than love if it's channelled positively.

It was only when I started working and earning money that I learnt to respect my father's best efforts. I realized how difficult navigating the real world was for me and thought it must have been the same for him too. Only then my relationship with him improved and stabilized.

What was your first job in films and what was it like?

MS: My first job was to go to a music company's office to collect cassettes and bring them back to our office. In the course of running around and doing odd jobs for my producer, I met Vikram Bhatt. I was seventeen then. Vikram said, 'You are a hard-working boy. I would like you to be my assistant director.' Mukesh-ji was present too and he said, 'Sure. Mohit, you should work with Vikram. He is a very talented director.' Vikram had already directed *Ghulam* (1998) and was in the process of directing *Dhun*, a TV serial.

I did not know then what the job of an assistant director was about. However, it paid Rs 500 more than what Mukesh-ji was paying me so I went for it. I needed money to be independent. Vikram's *Kasoor* was my first film as an assistant director, although at that time, I was clueless as to what the job necessitated.

That job defined my attitude and life thereafter. In the course of that job, I started feeling like a burden on the film set. I felt that the director and the unit were tolerating me only because I was the producer's nephew. Soon, there was an outdoor shoot scheduled in Switzerland and none of the other assistants were chosen for this shoot, except me. I thought I was the only one chosen to go because my uncle was the producer. I felt guilty that I was chosen over the others, as I was not working hard enough or knew as much as the others. However, I obeyed my producer and went for the outdoor shooting that was scheduled.

In those fourteen days of outdoor shoot, I worked sincerely and learnt a significant lesson as an assistant: there is no end to what a director can need while making their film. And assistant directors have an even bigger task than the director. Thereafter,

I did not wait to be told what to do next when I was on set. I became proactive and began thinking what else could be expected of me after I finished the task on hand. I can say this now: if you work with the attitude that you will act only when you are given orders by your superiors, you are no better than the furniture on the set. You have to take the initiative yourself, just like any good director does.

I think Vikram may have noticed my growth in that outdoor schedule because by the end of that shoot, he told me to work with him on another film, *Aap Mujhe Achche Lagne Lage* (2002). Thereafter, I worked as an assistant not to impress my uncle or my director, but to live up to my own standards, which I believe I had begun to raise with every job that I could lay my mind and hands on before moving on to the next one.

When did you first think you should direct a film?

MS: Emraan and I were returning to Bandra on a local train from a shoot of *Kasoor*. We were both assistant directors for that film. Emraan confessed, 'I don't think I want to be a director.' I said, 'I want to be a director only.' It was during this train journey that he decided he wanted to be an actor and I decided I would be a director. It's only when you live the process of film-making by being an assistant director that you begin to respect the role a director plays even more.

I realized, every single being associated with the film was looking only at the director for answers. A director had to be very good at human resources' management. A director leads, not just by answering the crew's questions but also by setting an example of their economic, management and administrative skills. My own experiences as an assistant director made me see my own directors, Vikram Bhatt and Mahesh Bhatt, in a different light.

I also realized that the assistant director's job is probably the most difficult job on the set, other than the lighting crew's, and yet I wanted to do it! That is what really attracted me to direction.

When did you take the leap of faith to direct your own film?

MS: I quit working with Vikram because I realized I would never become independent if I continued to work as an assistant, even though it paid very well. I began writing my script and doing odd production jobs for Vishesh Films, on and off. When *Tumsa Nahin Dekha* (2004) was in production and director Anurag Basu fell very ill, I was told to shoot the film. I think I shot for around thirty days. I was just twenty-one then!

On yet another occasion, during the making of *Footpath* (2003) when my director Vikram Bhatt's dates were not available because he was abroad, I was told to be present while the choreographer shot a song. However, there was a lot of chaos in the absence of the director, and the choreographer could not shoot for some reason. So, I was instructed to take over the shoot for that day. The shoot went well but I felt I had done a terrible job.

After the shoot, on my way back home, I was upset, worried that I had messed up the shoot, even though I had just shot one verse of the song. However, I got a call from my production man and he said, 'Mukesh-ji heard you did brilliantly well on the shoot today!' I was amazed. 'Are you serious?' I replied. Later I got to know that Bipasha Basu, the actor whom I had shot with that day, had called up Mukesh-ji after the shoot and told him, 'I told you this boy will do really well. And he is hard-working. He took over the shoot and if it was not for him, our dates would have been wasted.' I think her compliment must have given Vishesh Films a lot more faith to give me a film to direct when I was ready to direct one later. I thank Bipasha for her sincere recommendation.

How did you earn your first break as director?

MS: Mukesh-ji, Vishesh Films, was my producer. I wanted to direct a film but I was not sure where I wanted to go and when I wanted to make it. I got an idea and I started writing the story.

I was inspired from an English film I had seen, but had not written the story with the intention of directing it. But on hearing it, Mukesh-ji said, 'You have written it, you direct it.' I told him, 'I am not ready to direct a film.' He replied, 'You are never going to be ready to direct, unless you take the leap!' I think I was at the edge of the pond then and just needed a push. They threw me in and that's how I learnt how to swim. Before this, I had not shot anything independently neither for TV, TVC nor for a pop-song video. I just dived straight into directing my first film, because of their faith in me.

When you made Zeher, *did you ever feel it would've been helpful had you had a formal education in films?*

MS: No, but that actually made me keener to learn aspects of film-making while I was making my first film and others later.

Was the script of Zeher *a spontaneous act or did you keep box-office demands in your mind while writing?*

MS: It was my first film. I think I was too preoccupied approaching technicians and talents and asking, 'Sir/Ma'am, would you like to work in my film, I am a first-time director?' If they agreed, I was only too happy with that. No other thoughts occurred to me then. When I wrote *Zeher*, I simply wrote what I would have liked to see on screen. Even today, I cannot write thinking of what an audience will want to see.

In Aashiqui 2, the faith the girl has in her beloved was unwavering. Was her character a manifestation of your own need to have a relationship like that?

MS: Yes. Unconditional love is what we all look for in our lives. You may have noticed that in the story I have not given any importance to them getting married. They are not married in the film but still live together and share a deep bond. I do not think you need to be married to be together as soul mates. I married Udita one week after I finished shooting the film, and it were my two lead actors who pushed me to. So that film is a landmark event in my personal life. I thank my actors for doing this for Udita and me.

Share with us your experience of working with actors.

MS: There is no one way to work with actors. Generally, I try to imagine and also ask my actors, 'What if the scene had no dialogue? How would you have communicated the essence of that scene?' That, for me, is good directing. I try to bring out the potential of a person. Because I realized, very early in my career, if I try to learn acting myself to show an actor how to perform, they will be as good or as bad an actor as I am. And that might become outdated with time. Instead, it is better to let an actor show you what they can do.

I genuinely think a director need not be the best actor but their interpretation of a scene needs to be the best and they must be able to communicate that to the actor effectively. I believe we are capable of communicating effectively even without dialogue and only with body language. This is one of the things I concentrate on the most while extracting a performance from an actor.

In every film I try to cast one new actor. When you mix a combination of seasoned and new actors, it makes the overall performance dynamic. Therefore, I choose a variety of actors from various professional backgrounds and cast them together. I make it a point to cast a seasoned actor along with a VJ or a fashion model or a theatre/TV actor or even a rank newcomer.

Did you ever use illustration skills, like storyboarding, visualization skills for your first film?

MS: I had made a storyboard for my entire film. But, on the second or third day of the shoot, we realized that the production goods were stuck in traffic and if we waited for them, we would lose around three hours of shooting. We would lose the only day I had at that location. I decided not to wait for the storyboards I had made and began shooting, guided purely by instinct. That same day, post the shoot, I tore my shot division too. I decided to trust and go with my instincts. Ever since that day, I stopped making storyboards for my films.

Some directors believe the cinematographer is their best buddy on set. What do you believe?

MS: Not just buddies. I have always looked at the cinematographers as my elder brother. Whenever I feel down, they try to cheer me up and encourage me by telling me, 'No, you are a good director, hang in there.' When I lose my temper, they ask me to chill out. They have always cajoled me and taken care of me like a brother would.

Who was the cinematographer of your first film?

MS: Fuwaad Khan. I call him 'Bhai'. He had worked on *Jism* (2003) and *Murder* (2004) and had also worked with an array of new directors. So I decided to go with him. He was very encouraging. He is the kind of person who showed the least interest in what's going on when everything was falling into place really well but when there was a crisis, he was the best person to go to. A director facing a dilemma about any decision would cause him to suit up and try his best to make the shot great by using every camera or lighting technique possible.

If an actor had limitations and I felt that the shot or the scene would suffer because of that, I would confide in Fuwaad Bhai and he would say, 'Don't worry about it, I will put up a shot in such a manner that it will take the audience's attention away from the actor's shortcoming.' He was great in that sense. He never made me feel like a first-time director, never made me feel I was just a twenty-two-year-old.

Who was the editor of your first film?

MS: Aqeeb Ali. He is someone to whom I attribute a lot of my success. He and I started off as assistant directors with Vikram. After Vikram would edit his scenes, Aqeeb and I would edit the same scenes keeping in mind our differing perspectives, just to see what we could do with the same footage. We learnt a lot on the job.

When I saw the first rushes, I wanted to reshoot everything! Even now, after six films, I remember seeing the rushes of my last film and wanting to reshoot the whole thing. Honestly, if you ask me, even after a film is shot and ready, I have the energy and enthusiasm to start it all over again. This is where my producer plays an important role. He just tells me to shut up and stop indulging my fears. When my producers saw my first cut, they were delighted. Mukesh-ji took me out for dinner to JW Marriott. He said you deserve a great meal and drinks. They were so happy.

I learnt so much during my first edit. Earlier I was very much in love with shots, and only during the process of editing did I realize that it's not about a great-looking shot, but about the entire scene working in totality. I am no longer attached to the shots I take. If my editor or I feel that the shot is not helping but harming the scene, we get rid of it without any further delay.

Who was the art director of your first film?

MS: Rajat Poddar. And I am working with him even today. Rajat and I started off on a not-very-pleasant note when we were working on Anurag Basu's film. I was directing it only because Anurag was unwell and was arguing with Rajat on a decision we both had to take. Technically, it was not my film and we both had a different way of looking at it. I liked that he had a point of view, even if we argued over it. I liked that he stood by what he believed. We could agree to disagree about anything we discussed and that is where Rajat and I connected. A person who has a definite point of view invariably has a longer career, I believe. Even now, we have differences of opinion but we agree to disagree and look for solutions.

I think it is important to note that when you make low-budget films with newcomers, the director has a lot more work to do. Rajat has the skill to give me the faith that I am getting what I want within our budget without making me feel that I have made any compromises with respect to quality. There is this scene in *Awarapan*, where I told him I wanted something that makes the character recollect his past. He asked if we could bring back the shot of the doves for that so he wouldn't have to create any new art for that feeling. When I insisted otherwise, Rajat straight up said, 'No, you already have something more emotional than what I can make you; just use that again.'

How important is sound to you as a film-maker? Any unforgettable sound memory from your formative years?

MS: If you also include the score and songs as sound, I would say it contributes to much more than 60 per cent of your film. For me, sound should never be larger than the film or the visual. That is very difficult to achieve, because people have a belief that they need to make the loudest impression by using sound alone. I believe if sound or visual stand out more than the scene, the scene has failed. When I entered the profession, sound technology transitioned from stereo to Dolby. I realized people watching a film in a cinema hall reacted the same way to the sound as people watching the same film on a pirated CD. This proves that sound is more about being creative and less about being technical.

I still work with sound engineer Hitendra Ghosh, a very senior technician. When he remixes a scene, he keeps in mind the writing and the drama. He does not let sound overwhelm the script or the performance. We begin to tweak the sound for technique only when he has achieved the correct balance. I really enjoy the process of remixing post the film's production. Finally, whatever the technology and techniques, the camera, the visuals, the editing, the sound and any other element have to support the writing.

If you ask me about a sound-specific memory from my past, I still remember the silence in the room when my mother told me to remove my shoes wet from the rain. I remember the sound of the rain too.

What was the most humbling experience from your first film?

MS: Many! You have to let go of so-called vain inhibitions you have about yourself. You have to become very vulnerable. Even in your most embarrassing moments while directing, you have to stand your ground and bare your vulnerability. Your sad moments, the happy ones, all the anxieties and excitement of having a physical relationship with your beloved, your weakest moments, these are the things you have to make sure reflect in your writing, on the set, and eventually on screen. Everything you were guarding closely, holding on to, hiding, everything is out there! Your bravado and pride, your prejudices, your good, your bad, your selfishness, whatever is in you that makes you *you*, is bared to the people you work with, and your audiences too. That is what was most humbling for me.

Do you prefer a relaxed atmosphere or a stressed one?

MS: I am a sucker for stress! When things are going wrong, I am great. However, I do not consciously create stress. It happens naturally when I make things around me more challenging to accomplish.

When I shifted from film to digital, which is cheaper, the cinematographer was rolling the camera earlier than planned, the assistant signalling the start was clapping leisurely, people were walking in and out of the frame without caring that the camera was rolling. I did not enjoy shooting that day because there was no stress on me. I knew a retake wouldn't cost my producer raw stock and a lot of money. So I instructed everyone to recreate the feeling of film stock, to act as though we were using a film camera. The cinematographer was instructed to roll the camera only when I said roll, the clapper boy or girl was told to sound the clap and rush out of the frame—all of this was an attempt to create the atmosphere of us shooting on the more expensive film raw stock that would stress me out, hopefully. The shoot went well after that.

Would you say a film set is a place where a director has to manage egos?

MS: I would not term it ego management. A director needs to make everyone feel that they will or have found their true self while working on the film. Make them believe it's not just your [the director's] film, but theirs too. When you can make your technician or talent believe that they will or that they have done the best job they could, you are, in a way, transferring your ownership of the film to them. That is when they tend to deliver their best.

It's only when they feel what they are doing is not going to be their best work, that there might be an ego tussle between the director and the technicians/talents. Honestly, every human being has an ego. Use it to help the film. If you can make them believe you are not competing with them and they are not competing with you, that is using ego in a positive manner.

Are you upfront with your crew when you feel you are facing some confusion or limitation on set?

MS: I am honest about any limitation or dilemma when I face one. It takes more energy to conceal something than to reveal it. It also takes more time to conceal your uncertainty about something rather than being vulnerable and admitting it. If I do not have a reply when my cameraman, or any other technician, questions me about their technique or mine, I simply admit that I do not have a solution or answer as yet and am open to suggestions.

Why do you still wake up to the same dream, film-making?

MS: That is the one thing that stays with you. You get up every day thinking how you can do more and it is a great feeling. When nothing around you stays, somehow your films always stick with you. It is the greatest girlfriend, wife, buddy and companion you can have.

In front of the world we might portray ourselves as strong individuals who know everything. But, truth is, no one really knows anything for certain. Whoever thinks he has the perfect recipe for success and entertainment actually knows nothing. The fact is everyone is as unknowing and unaware as everyone else in the world. If you think film-makers know how life is to be lived better, you are wrong. No one has this information—not the gurus or the film-makers or the priests or the monks. The question, 'What should I do in life?' has no definite answer, which is good. You are just as lost after as you were before making a film.

In the future, if your child comes up to you and says they want to be a film-maker, what advice would you give?

MS: I have a long way to go before doling out advices to people. Yet, I would say, go and make your film. Do it your way. I will refrain from giving any specific advice, because whatever I say today might not hold tomorrow. My methods might not work or become outdated in the future. So they have to make their own unique journey. I honestly wish that they do not have to carry the baggage of being my son or daughter because I have seen a lot of people succumb to that pressure. You cannot be a film-maker by imitating somebody else. Not even your father. So, the more you detach from your film-maker father or mother, the better.

If I have to say something more to them, I would say, 'Get a camera and shoot.' It is the best way to find your voice and tell your own story. It will help you find what you feel and what you need to do to better your skills and build your talent. You could find that you need to read more books or go to a film school or assist a director. I am not against education but education need not always be attained via a school. I believe my assisting days were when I learnt the most.

I would give one tip: there is no big film or small film; no big or small break; no ideal first film; no ideal woman, ideal sex or ideal relationship; in the same way there is no ideal way for you to learn film-making or become a director, or actor, or business person, or anything else in life. Every director will tell you about certain paths they followed that made them film-makers.

You are interviewing many directors for your anthology, and in everyone's paths there will be some constants, but in each of them there will be a unique thing, one new thing they did, which made them film-makers. My child has to find that unique thing.

Is there any advice you would like to give someone who is starting new, in film-making or any other career?

MS: I would say trash everything you have read and heard so far and write a page of your own life. Then trash that too and the day after, begin writing about your life as it exists in that moment. You have, now, read about somebody in the past, which was you and learnt from their mistakes and successes. While you write, you will also read about your own life, with all its achievements and losses. Trash it and start afresh. Start writing afresh and start living afresh. Place an empty page in your mind and think about how, in a decade or so, you will write on this page, only to trash it and write all over again.

PERSPECTIVE FROM ANOTHER LENS

Cinematographer Ravi Walia speaks of Mohit Suri

Ideally, a cinematographer and a director must understand each other and develop a language together that allows them to read each other's minds. Developing that kind of camaraderie and that kind of communication with any director is great; I have that with Mohit. We have worked in three films so far, *Raaz 2*, *Crook* and *Murder 2*.

From our very first film together, I understood he was not the kind to unnecessarily interfere in my craft. I doubt he even told me how he wants to block a scene or light it, because somewhere somehow we had formed an understanding where I paid heed to his story while shooting it and he paid heed to cinematography and lighting in his vision for the film. We were on the same page ever since the first film and have been travelling on the same wavelength throughout all the films we have shot together.

Mohit, despite being a young director, is extremely skilled. I know of great storytellers but Mohit has the additional capability of utilizing his tools of direction to tell his stories in the way they need to be told. This makes the job of a cinematographer easier.

Mohit is a taskmaster. He provokes you to think and travel beyond his suggestions and references. He points me to a path, but wants me to take him to his destination, one beyond his imagination and reference. He's not happy with anyone who simply goes along with him, he likes people to go beyond him, his ideas and lead his moment and his shot to a better destination than he had imagined or suggested. He does that because he believes that as his cameraman it's my space and decision on how to achieve and go beyond his visual references. This is the space all cameramen crave from their directors. It's very challenging and fun for me, it keeps me on my toes and makes me try harder and do better than my best. On several occasions, I have worked with experienced directors who want exactly the reference they show you. Such assignments are not challenging and thus not intellectually or creatively stimulating.

When Mohit narrates the story or script to me, the first question he asks is, 'Did you like it or not? Does it interest you?' Now, that's a question that directors rarely ask us. This is an admirable quality because it shows he is open to criticism and suggestions from his cinematographer. If I tell him, 'Hmm, the story or script is just okay.' He will ask me what or which parts are not working and will be very interested in my answers. He listens to me if I want to speak up. He will discuss the nitty-gritty of the story if I want to discuss my reservations at a magnified level. That's how open he is to a cinematographer, a profession that some directors consider to be incredibly technical and who often tell us, 'As my cinematographer, it's your job to only light and shoot my scene, aim the camera correctly and speak only when spoken to.' This gives us the confidence that on set or location when stakes are running high, this director [Mohit] will be open to my ideas too that are born from my own vision and from my experiences. This makes working with him and dealing with the regular pressures of cinematography and film-making far easier to bear. This attitude of his helps me walk into the first shot on the first day with confidence due to the comfort zone established by someone I respect, trust and have faith in.

It is not that I have always been correct in my suggestions, sometimes they have not worked out and have been turned down by him but always with adequate explanations and reasoning. Therefore, I do not hesitate to offer my ideas and suggestions the next time. This helps create the camaraderie I mentioned earlier.

Freedom is important for us cinematographers, because we come onboard with our own experiences and our own knowledge and vision that we never intend to impose on the director. We want to provide another perspective, another path, to travel; one that may be beyond the director's own imagination and vision. Having said that, we do have to be complementary to the director's vision and be honest to the script. Mohit and some other directors

I have worked with tell me what they want and then leave it to me to achieve it or achieve more that it.

When Mohit arrives on set he usually asks me how I want to shoot the scene. He hears me out and either goes with what I'm saying or suggests something different. If I suggest that we should backlight the scene, he will stage the scene so that in the morning he shoots in the direction the sun is rising and then he choreographs the rest of the scene when the sun is setting so that I get the constant backlight I had suggested. He does not panic or get stumped if I say that we shoot something in a particular way. He adapts to things easily.

When I set up a shoot, Mohit will look at the frame and ask me the lens I've used. If I say it's a 35mm, and he wants to go wider, he will not tell me which ones to use for that purpose, he will just suggest that we should change the lens and go wider, even though he knows enough about lenses and could suggest the exact one. Furthermore, he doesn't instruct me to go wide, rather he suggests that we go wider. That's how polite and dignified he is.

Mohit is a passionate director and really good at utilizing the limited resources provided by his producer without compromising on the quality and the narrative. Sometimes I wonder how he will handle the money if he gets a very big-budget film. He works so hard that I feel he should take it a bit easy for the sake of his crew. But his crew is great and they can keep up with his passion. Seeing him work is inspiring for me, for anyone on his crew. He makes a good leader of the crew.

With Mohit, the preproduction is very important. He will discuss anything and everything about the script, the production, etc., at every possible level, so that when we go on shoot every technician and his assistants know what we are doing and why we are doing it. He is one of the directors who believes it is not the time for discussions when the lights are on. Have the discussions, the arguments, before we go on shoot. So he cares for the producer's money and the time and energy of his crew.

Another ability he has is he can choreograph the screenplay of his songs without his choreographer in case he is unavailable for some reason; it is something he has executed beautifully many times.

He does not mind if I or any other technician fail to execute what he wants, or fail to execute something that we suggested; what is very, and more important to him is that we first try to achieve what we want or what he wants. He keeps his cool, he has patience for mistakes . . . that is another great quality in him.

On a personal level, on the surface he may look aloof or disinterested or even snobbish, however that is a façade. He is deeply emotional and loves his solitude. I am not surprised his films are high on the emotion quotient, as those emotions that we see in his films, are there deep within him.

TANUJA CHANDRA

'Every artist has inside him a secret place. Only the great ones have the courage to go there.'

FILMOGRAPHY

Dushman (1998); *Sangharsh* (1999); *Yeh Zindagi Ka Safar* (2001); *Sur: The Melody of Life* (2002); *Film Star* (telefilm 2005); *Zindagi Rocks* (2006); *Hope and a Little Sugar* (2008); *Qarib Qarib Singlle* (2017)

SNEAK PEEK

Born in Delhi, Tanuja Chandra lived briefly in Hong Kong and has spent most of her life in Mumbai. She graduated in English literature and has a master's in film direction and writing from Temple University, US. She started her media career with Plus Channel, directing news and entertainment stories. She was also the editorial coordinator for a variety of shows. She directed her first TV series, *Zameen Aasman*, in 1995; worked in her first feature film, *Tamanna*, as a co-writer in 1997; followed by *Zakhm* (1998). She directed her first film, *Dushman* in 1998.

MY TAKE

I first met Tanuja Chandra nearly a decade after my father, who was the lyricist of *Dushman*, had passed away. I happened to run into her at a coffee shop near my house. At that random meeting, I introduced myself to her and we chatted as if we had known each other forever. She enthusiastically shared some of her experiences of working with my father. My father had casually mentioned an incident while working with her, during one of our dinner-table conversations, '[. . .] I think she was anxious that being a small-budget film, her producer may not be able to afford my writing fees. I asked her, "Who told you I work only for money, first tell me your film's story. That will also decide if we will work together." I heard the story and I felt challenged, uncertain and anxious if I would be able to do justice to it as a lyricist.' And on this note, began a brief but lovely friendship. I had just begun working as an assistant director in TV then and had written two episodes of a TV series, *Saboot*.

I learnt how important it is for any film-maker to, first and foremost, have a great story in place if they aspire to work with any creative talent who is considered a legend and/or a blessing for them on their film. A good story can win over anyone. Just as our grandparents or mothers won us over with some great tales when we rested on their laps. I guess, we never really change.

Post our conversation, I felt she is a friend I could seek advice from any day and I did ask her for some guidance while deciding upon this book's preface. She is a good listener, witty, happy-go-lucky, passionate, enthusiastic and spontaneous. A lot in a tiny package.

THE CONVERSATION

Rakesh Bakshi: *Thank you for being a part of this book. There is a dialogue in your first film,* Dushman, *I really liked, 'Jo baat dil se nikalti hai woh seedha asar karti hai [Words that stem from one's heart affect deeply].' Does it reflect the essence of being a writer, director and an actor?*

Tanuja Chandra (TC): I am very happy to meet you for your book. My parents always encouraged my siblings and me to read, so I value books. If people like us who are engaged in the arts absorb everything that is going on around us, it will enrich us, nurture us and end up in the work we do. The kind of writing that I connect with personally has something to do with the emotion of longing—somebody wanting something very badly and not getting it and fighting for it. The helplessness, the vulnerability, but not looking away from what you want—all the twisted scenarios of the heart, basically!

As for the dialogue you mentioned, it's almost a kind of storytelling mantra. It's as if one is telling the writer within or an actor one is interacting with, 'Give me a bit of your heart, do not give me a dialogue or performance.' Because in the movies, when an emotion is genuine and felt deeply, it will find a direct path to your audiences' heart. You pointed this to me in the dialogue, but I never realized until now that it is indeed my philosophy of work, be it writing or direction!

What was your childhood like and what were the 'creative' activities you were occupied with back then?

TC: I was born in Delhi. My father was transferred to a few places because he worked for a corporate, but I have spent most of my life in Mumbai. I studied in a convent, Villa Teresa High School, then we lived briefly in Hong Kong. After that I did my BA in English literature from St Xavier's College, during the time of legendary professor Eunice de Souza.

At home, my siblings and I always received genuine encouragement to pursue that which made us happy. When I was little, I hated movies. I used to believe that everything that was happening on screen was real! Even though my mom tried explaining the truth to me, it was a while before I got over it. Even now, I have to say, a film or a book that gets to me stays in my bloodstream for at least forty-eight hours.

Times of India used to have a middle-page column in which I often published my stories. That was in college. My ultimate dream then was to write a book, and I did, *Bijnis Woman: Stories of Uttar Pradesh*, which was published in March 2017. And I've quite regularly written pieces for magazines and websites over the years.

I also enjoyed taking black-and-white pictures with my Nikon SLR camera and my subjects were usually people. My sister, my friends. I loved taking pictures of faces. I think somewhere the need to be able to tell a story in one, still frame, was very much an interest even when it wasn't my profession.

In college, I enjoyed watching movies but never really thought I'd make them. It was only when I lived in the US and began making short films on the Indian community there, that I knew I wanted a career in films. Before that, I wanted to be a writer–journalist. I then joined a film school in Philadelphia before returning to India to be a part of the entertainment industry.

Do you have a first memory of a movie you saw?

TC: I think it started with a video tape of *Sholay*. After that, I began to think of movies as cool.

Do you have a first memory of wondering how they make movies?

TC: *Star Wars* and *E.T.* are movies I wondered about. These were magical and swept me away. I was young when I visited the lavish set of Raj Kapoor's *Prem Rog* (1982) with my mother, but I found it quite interesting. She was a first-time scriptwriter then.

Did you want to be a film-maker since childhood, considering your mother was a scriptwriter?

TC: I went to the US after my bachelor's, just to live and experience life there. To support myself, I taught kids in a school, while learning how to shoot and edit in a public cable company in Houston. That's when the bug bit me and I joined a master's programme in film-making at Temple University, Philadelphia. I returned and began working in TV. My first job was with software producer, Plus Channel, under Amit Khanna. They produced video magazines for which I directed and edited stories. All this earlier work in television helped me reach my goal of film direction.

In film school, there seemed to be a tendency to exist in a bubble, making films for other students and a handful of teachers to evaluate, not a real audience. Producing for TV means aiming to entertain actual viewers, working against competitors. If you cannot engage an audience, they will switch to something else. The chemistry between the audience and a story is unique, something in which the maker has no part to play. Plus Channel in many ways was my real film school. It built the practical structure on top of the theoretical foundation I already had from film school.

Since childhood, I've always felt strongly about social ills and prejudices around me, so I guess I organically veered towards those kinds of stories. When my mother saw *Tamanna*, a film I co-wrote, she said, 'Now I know you can take care of yourself.' She used to worry, as mothers often do about this line of work, about its unpredictability. But after *Tamanna*, she could see this is what I loved doing and she wholeheartedly endorsed it. That felt good.

I was primarily interested in fiction and it was very exciting to begin work in the TV serial, *Zameen Aasmaan*, written by the great Manohar Shyam Joshi around 1996. I began by controlling the crowd on outdoor shoots and was chief assistant in the first ten episodes and then took over as the director. The director did not want to continue any more and everybody on the team decided I should take over. For me, that was a huge promotion. That was my first solid, directorial job.

I believe I was offered this first independent direction because I had been a proactive assistant. I did everything—no job was small for me. From rehearsing lines with actors to transporting video tapes, to instructing the cameraman, to transcribing, scheduling and even creating an easy-to-decipher library of shots for the editor, I did it all. Everything was my job and you wouldn't have heard a 'no' from me for anything. 'The more you do, the more you learn,' has always been my firm belief.

Thereafter, I co-wrote *Tamanna*, my first feature film, with Mahesh Bhatt, after which I co-wrote *Zakhm*, for which I was also an associate director. That was the final film he directed and it was an extremely treasured experience of my life.

When did you first approach a producer with the subject of Dushman?

TC: During *Zakhm*, I worked very closely with the actor and producer of the film, Pooja Bhatt. I would often direct her. Naturally, I got to know her well. So, when I stumbled upon a story that interested me to make as my first feature, I approached her. While *Zakhm* was still being made, I narrated the story of *Dushman* to her. She immediately said, 'Let's make it!'

At the time, Mahesh Bhatt had decided he would stop directing. He was keen to nurture younger talent and *Dushman* happened. Years later, I directed *Sur* for Pooja Bhatt, which was her first production independent of the parent company, Vishesh Films.

How did you get the stars onboard, Kajol and Sanjay Dutt? Because getting stars onboard helps a film get the green light.

TC: Thanks to Mahesh Bhatt, I met Sanjay Dutt, who is a warm, genuine person. He said, 'I am happy to do this film for you.' He and I got along famously; I adored him. He does things from his heart, he never once gave me a hard time. In fact, he poured himself into the role of the blind major. Kajol said yes to me after the very first script-sitting! She's an equally genuine person and has a streak of adventure. She follows her instincts and is a really fine person with a strong character.

Do you conduct script rehearsals, workshops for actors during preproduction?

TC: I totally believe in doing readings, workshops and rehearsals with actors before shooting. During my early films, however, this wasn't much of a practice. At the time, directors met with actors for a narration, followed this with some discussions on the script, chat some more during costume trials, and then move straight to the set. So, as it was done then, actors would appear on my set, learn the lines, block the scene with me, rehearse with each other and shoot. Of course, a lot of preparation would have been done by me before this, which can be considered a kind of workshop, but on the set another kind of energy would take over. There is spoken and a lot of unspoken communication— much of direction is unspoken; it's a strong emotion felt by the director that is understood not so much in words but in feeling by the actor.

Doing workshops with your actors is great because everyone gets familiar with the script and also in a sense, this compensates for the absence of formal studies or intensive training of actors in this country. Even though I don't like over-rehearsing scenes, the actors get to know each other and what I'm seeking from them.

How does all of that help you while directing them on set?

TC: Workshops can rarely be as deadly as the real thing. When the lights are burning, the camera's moving, and it's, 'Take time,' the energy is just of a different kind. It's all live. That said, a heartfelt rehearsal can come quite close. Also, there is brainstorming, intense debating and this makes the script evolve. And then the really magical stuff happens on set when an actor goes beyond the director's brief, when he feels a moment in its absolute, raw urgency. When there is nothing between him and his emotions. And this can't be rehearsed. It is a happy accident. Like life.

Sometimes actors arrive on set having rehearsed a scene in a certain way in their minds. And if that's different from the way the director has envisioned it, it's often difficult to break that preconceived notion. Then they can get stuck in a loop. When that happens, I feel very sorry for them and helpless too because I'm pushing one way and they're going another. That's when your direction and their performance, both, possibly fail. Workshops help you to go through the entire script with the actors, mindful of the vision of the director. Theatre actors are the true workshop people. The rigorous rehearsals break the actor down, and in a sense, rebuild them, to become the character that the director had in mind.

Which was the first film where you began doing script-readings or workshops with actors?

TC: For *Sur* we did readings with both Lucky Ali and Gauri Karnik. She spent time learning how to mimic playing the violin. For *Hope and a Little Sugar*, we did readings too. Now the blocked dates of actors include workshop time along with the shoot dates (and, of course, dates for promoting the film). And when you work with newer actors, it is easier to get them to commit time for rehearsals.

With which actor/s and films did you do no workshops or readings but they gave you a dream performance?

TC: I only narrated revisions of the script to Kajol to keep her updated but we didn't do readings. And she had a double role! Yet, hers was surely an amazing performance in *Dushman*. The same goes for Sanjay Dutt and Akshay [*Sangharsh*]. I believe, 'directing actors' is a skill that can be taught and honed. There is a course on directing actors I have attended at a film school in Amsterdam.

How would you elaborate on this skill?

TC: There is a skill but it's somewhat hard to define. Most of the time it's not the words you're using to direct the actor, instead it's an intense vibe that is reaching out to them. It's a physical charge. It's a most curious kind of intimacy. A good actor listens keenly, without a constant dialogue running in their heads; he or she surrenders, always willing to take it in, soak it in, drink it in. Listening with your mind and your body is a very important quality. And then the actor's body switches on like a light. One of my favourite directors, Ang Lee, [*Life of Pi*] said that he doesn't look at an actor's work as a performance, but as a 'revelation'. In other words, don't act, reveal. Reveal a bit of your soul. There is something to be said for any director who is able to bring that out in an actor.

Some directors, particularly some first-time film-makers, feel overwhelmed, when they are working with an actor who comes onboard with the conviction that a good director will have an answer to every question posed about the script, the costume, anything related to film. How did/do you fare at such times, particularly when an actor wants to know everything about the character and script?

TC: I really admire the kind of dedication it takes when actors begin thinking, feeling, walking, eating like their characters. I love it! And this 'personal' kind of workshop is supremely significant. We don't think before we behave like ourselves, do we? An actor also shouldn't need to 'try' to be the character, it should come to them organically. Of course, it's not necessary to know *everything* about the character, we hardly know everything about ourselves. So, while the actor and the director are intimately aware of most things about a character, the element of surprise should always remain. Even actors like Daniel Day Lewis, who for months before the shoot will only talk in the way the character talks, must,

I'm sure, not feel like he has exhausted the process of knowing the character. Even he, though completely in command of the way Abraham Lincoln walked or smiled, must have left parts unknown, bits left to chance.

Sometimes an actor will tell you, 'My character will not do this or say this.' At times, this may be true but not always. Because in life, we often say and do things that aren't consistent with our personality. That is how human beings are. Nobody knows everything, nobody can know everything. No performance must be perfect; in fact, for me as a director, it gets really interesting when an actor stumbles, fumbles, goes breathless, has helplessness all over their place trying to rectify the shot, because they may think they're badly messing up but sometimes, instead of it looking bad, it actually looks very natural and real. It's life unfolding right there, in front of you, and I feel so lucky to be there when it happens!

Christopher Hitchens has said that instead of being the man who tells the world how to live, a man who is certain of things, he would rather be the man who is unsure of everything, greedily soaking in life around him, always absorbing, always learning. I believe, that is what actors should do. And directors too. They should put in their best effort but never be too certain of anything they are doing. Where's the fun in that, yaar?

Who were the talents you worked with on your first film who you felt were a blessing considering you were a first-time film-maker?

TC: Well, first of all, Mahesh Bhatt himself! Such a wonderful director, such a consummate storyteller. My early boss; I've learnt so much for him. But besides him, in *Dushman*, I worked with some great craftsmen, whom I met through Mr Bhatt, but with each of whom I formed a solid, working relationship. One was writer Sachin Bhowmick, the other was my editor Waman Bhonsle. And never to forget the legend, Anand Bakshi. It was so enriching for me as a first-timer to work with people who are of an earlier era but in great form. These were stalwarts. I got along extremely well with them because I worked with them with the highest respect, never behaving like a young upstart who thinks she's too cool for them!

Sachin Bhowmick had a huge library of knowledge and scripts he had written; he was a very well-read person. Very often, during screenplay discussions, he would have scenes pop out of the novels he had read. Anand Bakshi, I cannot talk enough about! Bakshi Sahab was gentle, humble and yet, a very passionate person. His lyrics said so much about him and his values, his worldview. I feel if I were to ask him, 'Bakshi Saab, *apne baare mein kuch bataaiye* [tell us something about yourself],' he would have probably said, '*Bataane ke liye kya hai?* [what's there to tell you?]' But his songs would tell you what kind of man he was, they would give you an idea of the grand stature of his heart! *Kuch reet jagat ki aisi hai, harr ek subah ki shaam hui. Tu kaun hai, tera naam hai kya, Sita bhi yahan badnaam hui* [. . .] *Waah!* (And hundreds of songs like that.) And he gave me his heart on *Dushman*, making me feel bigger, more important than I was. He is one of the most prized experiences of my life.

I also greatly treasure knowing and working with M.M. Kreem [M.M. Keeravani], the genius music director and lovely man. We first associated with each other in *Zakhm* and then he made beautiful songs for me in *Sur*. The superb lyricist, Nida Fazli—it was an undeniable pleasure working with him, learning from him. During *Tamanna*, I got to know the great Kaifi Azmi, courageous writer and human being. Luminaries, all.

So many people I have worked and interacted with have given me much to cherish. It's amazing how each contribution in your life, big or small, affects you. Often people go away from your life or you lose touch with them, but their contribution stays with you, in the way you conduct your life, in the stories you tell. And often you cross paths with them again, and a whole new chapter begins!

I've had two perfect angels, my parents, who have given me more than can be put into words. Absolute, irrevocable, unchangeable support and love. My brother and sister, and my sister's children who are the love of my life; although you'd call these personal relationships, they have often seeped into my work and the stories that have interested me; they have all been important influences. I have childhood friends who have walked with me for decades.

People like Mahesh Bhatt, with whom I began my film career, will always be special for being the first person who thought I had talent. He was so encouraging, so much fun! Also, he introduced me to *his* teacher, U.G. Krishnamurti, who was so kind and wonderful to me. The stalwart-lyricist I had the good fortune to work with, Anand Bakshi, who was so appreciative even though it was just one film we did together, sent his grandson, Aditya, to assist me after *Dushman*. Much before this, my English professor in college, Eunice De Souza, my yoga instructor, Deepika Mehta, and many others have been people whose teachings will always stay with me. There are countless people who remain in the shadows, who have touched me deeply with their affection. It's startling, really, how much love one receives in one's life, which in turn informs one's work. In fact, it wouldn't be an exaggeration to say that I've learnt from everyone, even those who have been less than gracious.

How was your first day of shoot on Dushman? *Which scene did you shoot?*

TC: I will never forget it. I was extremely excited; the shooting shift was from 9 a.m. and the first shot was taken at 9.15 a.m.! (Let me make it clear here: my practice from my television days been to arrive on location an hour in advance.) We were shooting in south Bombay, around Bhendi Bazaar area, the scene in which Kajol is on her cycle, being chased by the villain. It was extremely challenging shooting in a real location; by noon, the crowds got unruly and uncontrollable. Kajol could not take it any more—people shouting, pushing, shoving, frightened her and the heat exhausted her. She left the shoot early. I tried to make her stay but it was just too much for her.

Bhatt Saab asked me what in the world made me schedule the first day of shoot in that kind of a crowded area. Well, to me, a real location is exciting as hell. It has the imprint of real life that just cannot be duplicated on sets. Crowded situations have never frightened me and I have shot in such places for many of my films. That day Mahesh Bhatt and Mukesh Bhatt really admired me for the way I handled the situation. I did not pack up when my main actor left. I continued shooting the villain's shots of chasing her. We did solo shots of him till pack-up time, even though my assistants were going crazy controlling the maddening crowds. I came away feeling my first day in a film shoot was a most fulfilling one.

On the first day of shoot, do you normally choose to shoot a difficult scene or an easier one?

TC: Never easy! In fact, I do not like beginning with easy stuff. I like to start with something I may have to wrestle with, something that may defy all logic. Then you start the relationship with your film shoot on a mad, passionate note.

So you prefer to be overwhelmed from the first day itself?

TC: I have really not been overwhelmed ever! I can deal with just about anything. I take crisis in my stride on a good day. And on a bad day, I may lose my temper a bit, but I make sure we finish what we had come for. Of course, we cannot be certain about everything; as a film-maker, one should expect some sort of problem all the time, some kind of mess each day, and then just deal with it as ably as possible. Yes, there'll be a day when a problem may be insurmountable, but I know that I'll try hard as hell to fix it before calling off a shoot. In this, one's team and the solidarity of the team matters most. I love my crew. In a no-holds-barred kind of way. It's teamwork that survives crises and not the director's mad drive alone.

Was there any event during your first film that really boosted your confidence as a first-time film-maker?

TC: There might have been many actually, I don't really recall a specific one. In one's first movie, one is quite reckless and fearless and it's a good thing to have that attitude. During my first film, I never fished for compliments, I was too busy getting my hands dirty! So, when appreciation would come it would surprise me. But I'd feel good thinking that if the established stars I was working with and my experienced producers were telling me that they liked what I had done, I must have done it right. One feels validated with appreciation, because deep down we are all looking for it. Of course, it's a momentary thrill, as it should be.

But if I have to answer you, I would say, there was a part of the climax, after Kajol kills Ashutosh Rana, when I wanted her to fall on the ground and let out a huge, uncontrolled cry. Kajol said she couldn't do it, it felt fake to her. She offered to cry a little. I told her that her character's long, tough journey had come to an end; at this point, her cry had to sound like an animal's wail. It needed to be terrifying, it had to jolt the people watching. She sceptically asked me to show her what I wanted.

I said okay and I fell to the ground and just unleashed myself in that one moment. I let out an anguished, painful cry. I was unselfconscious, unaware of what I was doing. Sanju was lying on the floor, I just held him tight and wept loudly. Everyone on set stopped what they were doing and just watched me cry, loud, heaving sobs. A minute or two later, I stopped. I looked at her, breathless and panting. She nodded, said she would do it as I wanted and then did a great shot. I was happy. I felt like a director of substance that day!

How important is storyboarding? Did you storyboard your first film?

TC: Storyboarding is a big help in getting clarity for yourself as a director and then communicating it to the rest of the crew as well. At a basic level, it helps you use somebody else's mind to illustrate your thoughts so that they aren't confined just in your own head. When you are telling a storyboard artist, 'This is how I see the scene,' they draw what they understand of your story and it is fantastic to see that perspective. Sometimes, you may not agree, but alternatively, you may find something truly beautiful.

Because of my unbreakable rule of coming to a shoot an hour early, I'm able to discuss the shot breakdown with my assistants, chat and exchange some positive vibes and basically warm up for the day ahead. This ensures the movie is clear in everyone's head, not just in yours. It's amazing how much better a day goes if you just arrive early for a shoot. It's simple, but it works.

That said, it isn't too great to get totally stuck in the way one has visualized scenes. Sometimes it's nice to leave some room for any kind of creative combustion that may happen. Actors wanting to do something a certain way, the cameraman wanting to try something unusual, or maybe one's assistants suggesting something—this is all good. So many energies all rushing into each other! Be open to something growing out of that; why be secluded in your own ivory tower? A storyboard should be a guide, not a cage.

Who was the cinematographer on Dushman?

TC: My DOP in *Dushman* was Nirmal Jani. Back in 1998, cinematography still retained the kind of old-world romance of soft focus, beautiful and bright images as opposed to darker, sharper, more realistic frames that are popular now. Digital photography is more sharp and is good with available light.

Nirmal Jani draws you to the faces he shoots, to the beauty of their features. He was a wonderful colleague, a very sweet person with whom I did two more films after this, both of which were different in their camerawork. DOPs can often be temperamental; he's the quieter sort, a simple man.

The DOP and director must create a world-vision together. You cannot let a conflict become more important than the resolution of the conflict. This is a marriage that has to necessarily work! I've had different kinds of DOPs. There was one who was so quick in lighting that he would be ready before the actors and I had finished rehearsing and would start reading a book! And then I had one who would take forever because he wanted nothing less than perfection. A wise DOP will keep constraints in mind. I don't push aggressively, I'm a gentle pusher. If a shot cannot have the lighting of the DOP's dreams, it can be as close to the dream as possible. There was one DOP who was confused, he kept changing the lighting. He would put up all the HMIs he had and then say, 'This is over-lit,' and start removing the lights one by one! We lost quite a bit of time. But most often, I'll use love, warmth and humour to move things along. I won't hesitate to say, 'Please help me, I'm losing time!'

In my most recent film, *Qarib Qarib Singlle,* I had a young, amazingly focused DOP (Eeshit Narain) who had beauty as well as time limitations in mind. It was a film about a journey, not the easiest kind to shoot and there was so much loveliness to capture in the landscape, but without a lot of time in which to do it. My DOP was of invaluable help in meeting the set goal.

How do you associate with cinematographers generally?

TC: I ideally like the DOP to be an associate director. I always come prepared but I would be extremely happy if the cinematographer would set the camera and create a frame according to how he sees the scene. But for this the DOP needs to be half a director himself! I've had pretty fulfilling work equations with my cinematographers.

It's good to cultivate a relationship of laughter with your technicians. Professionalism doesn't always equal seriousness. I think laughter often diffuses the pressure and loosens people up. Every now and then, we should break the tension with big laughter. I know I do it often enough!

Who was the editor on Dushman?

TC: Waman Bhonsle, an amazingly experienced technician who had edited about 150 films! It was my first and last film edited on the Steinbeck and it was fascinating working with him. I love the editing process. It's when the whole film comes together as a story.

I love to follow my editor's vision. My boss, Mahesh Bhatt, had suggested Waman Saab's name to me and said, 'He is very senior and may not be your type because you are young. Often, he may not speak the same language but he will guide you superbly and will edit with feeling and affection.'

I am so happy I took Bhatt Saab's advice, because I was completely amazed by this man performing his magic on my first film. He was thrilling to watch. I still remember a time I found a certain scene boring; I wondered if it were the writing or the direction that wasn't working. Waman Saab smiled a really cool smile and said the problem didn't lie in that particular scene. He went two or three scenes before the scene in question and made a couple of simple cuts in them and then he played them all in sequence. Magically, the boring scene no longer bored me! Waman Saab taught me that it's not necessary to edit a scene that appears slow. The problem could be lying in a scene much earlier. That was his genius! What a lesson I learnt from him. This is why editing is considered the final 'rewrite' of the script.

An editor can affect the destiny of a film. And you must allow the editor to go where his imagination takes him. If you do not allow the editor to do that, you are actually missing out on the possibilities of your own work. Sometimes shooting can be sketchy, especially when you have a limited budget. A director cannot be a genius who knows everything all the time; directors make mistakes. An editor often corrects these mistakes, and more importantly, if there is something buried in the subtext of the drama, and a sharp editor follows his or her heart, something special can be brought out. It may not be the way you have shot it but it'll enhance the film. So let them do their stuff and let them find the core of the movie. I've always found this to be true, right down to my most recent film and each time it fascinates me, even fills me with a kind of joy.

How did you react to the first edit, the first cut?

TC: The first time I watched *Dushman* as an edit, we saw only about an hour of the film as the shoot was still a work in progress. Honestly, I was kind of confused. I felt that there was a good tension in the beginning and then the film moved into a love story and the main tension dissipated. I wondered if it was going in the right direction. The good thing was that there was still over an hour of the film left to shoot. Waman Saab had given us a very good idea of where the film was heading. Many of the problems were then addressed in the scenes that were left to shoot. Mid-course correction can be so useful but it's only possible if the whole film isn't being shot at a stretch. In which case, one should edit on location while the shoot is going on to be able to feel the pace and tone of the film.

Who was the production designer and/or art director on Dushman?

TC: Production designer and art director weren't two heads at that time. Earlier, it was just an art director with a strong associate. I had met Sameer Chanda, the hugely talented and popular art director during my television days. He did art for my serial, so naturally he was the one I approached for my first film. Sadly, he worked in *Dushman* only for the first schedule, he set the tone for the look of the film, which was then very ably followed by Mr Bhatt's regular art director, Gappa Chakraborty.

Sameer Chanda created Kajol's house, which was simple but had bright colours and a certain femininity, since it was a house that had only female residents. And Sanjay Dutt's house, he made more masculine and unusual, with a tree right in the middle of the living room, which grew right through the roof! There was also a life-sized bird-cage, which provided a cool, ambient sound. He placed a net on the side of the staircase because a blind man would need that. It was thoughtfully and adventurously done by Sameer Chanda, who is someone I still admire and warmly remember after his unfortunate demise some years ago.

While dealing with so many different souls on a set, is direction also a kind of ego management?

TC: Yes, of course! There are many fragile hearts on a set, many fearful ones. There is always anxiety, often actors may be struggling with some kind of failure, and that can be difficult to manage. A bleeding and bruised ego can be more troublesome then a healthy, bloated one. Doubt only creates more doubt and that's really tough to handle. On the other hand, a successful star often thinks he knows best, and may feel the need to impart advice too often!

See, everybody who collaborates with you has a separate life that they are living. They only arrive on your set to do their job on your film and leave, including actors. You have to endeavour to make their best sides come out when they step out of their lives, into yours for however brief or long a time. Outside of the film set are contentious relationships, health issues, problems with children's school grades, a parent who's not well—there is no shortage of problems in life! Often, an actor or a technician is in the throes of battling these issues, and takes it out on the film crew. A director has to take care of such troubled people. That's why I'm committed to making my team feel and know that they are of great importance to me and the project. I push hard, but I'm not stingy with my compliments and affection. I've mostly adored my team members and had fun with them while working very, very hard as well. With every film, I've formed some lifelong relationships. Could anything be cooler than that?

Can direction be physically and emotionally exhausting?

TC: Absolutely. I start losing weight about a week into a shoot! Direction is a terrible job to be in. You should do it only if you're madly in love with it. You are committed to a project for a couple years at least, often more, if you're also the scriptwriter. And really, parts of the story are moments you've lived with all your life. At no point can you divorce yourself from this commitment because an incomplete project will amount to an immense loss of faith and reputation for you. One's self-esteem takes a beating in this profession all the time whether an actor, producer or director, but the director has been steering the ship for longer. You are practically married to a film and if at the end of the years of efforts, it fails, well, you feel the deepest sorrow.

Billy Wilder said, 'A director must be a policeman, a midwife, a psychoanalyst, a sycophant, and a bastard!' I add to that, 'A clown, a masochist, a tightrope walker and an absolute fool!'

I find your films immensely thought-provoking; do you feel you make movies to raise questions or answers?

TC: I like to make movies that ask questions about the world we live in. But I try to do this with an innocence and if possible, a sweetness. Not like some wise soul who has a deeper understanding of life than my neighbourhood street vendor or anyone at all for that matter. And I try not to have the movie arrogantly have all the answers. Who wants to end up giving a big speech that no viewer is interested in watching! Plus, I can only give my answers, which may not be everyone else's. But raising questions and questioning social rules, ethics, values, is a healthy exercise that movies must indulge in and this need not be a boring moral science lesson. In my last film, the questions were about love and relationships — in the life of a thirty-five-year-old woman, for whom it's not love the first time around. Who finds herself falling for a strange but unique guy for whom this is the fourth time around! This was a romcom, so questions about life can be like life—unpredictable, unknowable, filled with laughter and tears.

There is a dialogue in Hope and a Little Sugar, *'Son, you want to be an artiste, well every artiste inside him has a secret place, but only the great ones have the courage to go there.' Would you like to elaborate on this?*

TC: I believe, there's a place within a person's heart, a quiet place, where some kind of deep longing exists, grappling to understand human emotions and pain, aching to achieve brilliance and happiness, trying to live a full life. This is something I try to bring out in my characters, my movies.

All creative people try to excavate this secret place within but only the great ones actually unearth their true selves, struggle with their inadequacies and failures, take risks that can ruin them, kill them even. You may seemingly be the happiest person on earth, the most successful, the most beautiful, but there will be a longing in you as a human being for connection, for belonging. A longing to truly belong to yourself, to really have an intimacy, to truly taste life. Although great artistes over the ages, including your father, have realized it's really quite impossible to achieve this, to even comprehend this longing or to put it into words. Which is why we all try so hard to touch the heart of the matter, in movies, books, poetry.

In 2008, you had a film that might not have made it to the box office 'hit' list of the year and after nine years, you've made a film that received huge critical acclaim as well as love from audiences all over. What occupied your life in the 'gap' years?

TC: I've been asked this question so much with the assumption that between releases, a director does *no* work! I was busy writing scripts, pitching them to producers and actors—two of these were on the verge of being made but then got stalled, for various reasons. I was at the time also working on the script of *Qarib Qarib Singlle* and this got made!

Unlike actors who work on several movies in a year and producers too, directors can't do that. Most often, directors do one film in several years. Especially if one is a writer–director. For most people, getting actors onboard and shooting a film is the only noticeable sign of work. When in fact, so much that goes before and after is possibly even more work. Especially when a lot of effort is invested in projects, but sadly, they don't always reach the stage where they become visible to people, a 'gap' is spoken of. This time is the necessary commitment required by a director and that's what I was doing. Luckily, scripts are like gold. They are never a waste of time. They are of high value and can be used at any time, the scripts I have from this time are very much there for me to revive later.

And notably, I had a book published in 2017, my first! This was a life-goal and I'm very happy to be a published author. It's a book of short stories from Uttar Pradesh, and very close to my heart. And even before I began work on this book, I was working on another one, a more challenging one, a novel. I hope to finish that soon.

Is film-making a journey or a destination?

TC: I do not think film-making can be a destination when the thing it speaks of is itself a journey! At best, film-making is the intention to create a body of work you can be proud of, despite its flaws and shortcomings. Don't forget—films, books, poems, all endeavours, including the creation of buildings and bridges— these outlive the creators. There is something to be said for leaving behind something that can bring value to peoples' lives long after one is gone.

Every film is a learning experience and there are things you did not know one film earlier, which you do now. And there are things you'll know only after you make the one you're about to! The crucial thing is to keep updating one's knowledge. A person will be left behind if they don't keep up with the latest stories, films, styles, technology. I try to keep myself abreast of what is happening in the world of films as well as the real world. Everything you've learnt in life and whatever you've lost, most of it finds its way into your writing. Even your tragedies, your sorrows, your tears benefit you by becoming scenes in your film, your book, your television show. Thank goodness for that, otherwise there's not much to be said for sadness!

If your child or niece/nephew says to you they want to get into films, what advice would you offer them?

TC: I would say, 'By all means, go ahead!' We must never come in the way of peoples' dreams. I would not be able to spare them their share of difficulties that come with film-making, but then I wouldn't also be able to ignore the joys that would come their way. I think the only advice I would give, would be this: 'Work with the deepest integrity. And do not let anything break you, there will be lows but you will recover from them for sure. And equally, when you do get success, do not think you have arrived and you know more than everybody else because there will always be somebody who knows more than you.' Lastly, I would say, be civil, be honest, build relationships and always have faith.

I always say this to anyone who wishes to make movies or any other creative job, do *all* work, do any work. Do not feel you are too smart, too special. Start with doing the smallest job of running from one place to another, take part in all activities, in all departments. All of it will teach you. You have to take in life buzzing all around you, only then will you have material to create the building blocks of storytelling.

Anything you would like to share with the youth today? What's important for them to have?

TC: *Imaandari* [Honesty]! *Jo bhi kaam karo, imaandari se*, there should be incorruptible integrity towards work, towards people.

You may not be the most skilled person in the world or the most creative, but as long as you have done it with full imaandaari, not cheating yourself or anybody else, no lying or dishonesty to yourself and others, it will be a fulfilling and successful experience. And there will be a tone of respect for you, because people know when a person doesn't lie.

Last but not the least: empathy and compassion. There's a memorable incident from my childhood, which defines my father's nature and values and has definitely influenced me throughout my life. Just a small image, really. My father is from a small town in UP, called Badaun. When we were little, we often visited his home. We used to take a bus from Bareilly to Badaun. I remember one such bus journey, when a passenger seated next to my father fell asleep, mouth open and all, his head totally resting on my dad's shoulder. My sister and I gestured to my dad to wake up the fellow and ask him to sit straight, but my dad whispered that he didn't mind it, to let the fellow be, as he was resting. My father would not disturb a sleeping co-traveller! I still smile remembering this. To me it has remained an enduring image of empathy towards a complete stranger. These gestures of kindness make us human. They may be small, but their importance is tremendous.

PERSPECTIVE FROM ANOTHER LENS

Cinematographer Nirmal Jani speaks of Tanuja Chandra

I have done three films with Tanuja, *Dushman*, *Sur* and *Hope and a Little Sugar*. Tanuja was the associate director on Mahesh Bhatt's *Zakhm*, so I knew her when she approached me to photograph her first film. When I heard the story of *Dushman*, I felt this seemingly small-sized woman had a raging fire in her to tell a story and make a film. I felt that from day one. Such is the passion with which she works on her films.

I knew at once that the film she was making was unusual and different from what I had done so far. Women directors are few in our industry, so it was a good opportunity for me to work on a subject like this.

On reading the script, I knew two elements were very important in the film: one, the audience must feel scared of Gokul, the evil and psychotic serial rapist and murderer, when they see him; and second, the death of Kajol's twin sister must impact the audience emotionally. That is what she wanted too. So, I felt I was in tune with the director on these two significant issues in the story.

I discussed what kind of lighting and lensing the film needed so that every shot could convey the story she wanted to narrate. Even the silent moments in the film should convey the meaning and impact of the moment, the drama via the lighting, the camera lensing and the placement of the camera, angle, etc. Those days, there was no video-assist and no DI, so I had to show her the frame through the viewfinder and create the mood and tone on the set or location itself. I would always insist, not only with her but even with other directors, that they must see the rehearsal of the scene through the viewfinder of my camera. Because what she views now is what the audience will watch too. I was glad she trusted me because complete trust between the director and the cinematographer is very important.

Tanuja would rehearse the scene either with the artists or her assistants, and we would block it accordingly. She is excellent with actors. She would even act the scene to tell them what she wanted. You have to understand, a star like Kajol was working in the film and she is one actress who will not do anything for you unless she believes in you or the story behind the scene you want her to do. So you have to be a very refined director to be able to handle a star like her. Even though it was her first film, she handled Sanjay Dutt and Kajol skilfully and competently. But not just the stars, she also directed a new actor like Ashutosh Rana capably. That is a sign of a very good director: their ability to handle raw talent and a star together.

I remember when we were shooting Ashutosh's first appearance in the film, Tanuja took me aside and said, 'First impression is the last impression. This scene is the first time the audience is going to see this character, Gokul. I want you to shoot it, light it, lens it, whatever you have to do, in such a manner that the audience not only gets shivers on seeing him but never forgets his demonic personality for the next two hours.' This tip was very helpful to understand the significance of this character and the effect his visual was supposed to have on the viewers. That is why I consider her a good director, she explains the characters and drama so well that it makes me understand how I can present it to her on film. Once I set up the shot I usually ask her if that was what she had in mind. Sometimes I get it right, and sometimes I don't. When I get it wrong, she explains exactly how she sees it so I can make the necessary changes.

The other time Tanuja really impressed me was when she directed the song, '*Chitthi Na Koi Sandesh*', when Kajol's twin sister is dead. For me that was a scene, not a song, and yet she worked on the choreography of the moments of that scene and the camera movement so well, with very slow forward tracks of the camera on a dolly and long static shots of the body in the living room. Even the lyrics of the song complemented the screenplay so beautifully that it made me and many others in the cinema hall cry. She is very good at handling and presenting emotions, and I think it's mostly because she feels things so deeply and can therefore handle the deepest of matters, emotions, relationships, issues, capably.

She has handled different genres of films ably. For example, the films I have done with her: *Dushman* was a thriller, *Sur* was a musical, and *Hope and a Little Sugar* was a drama involving racism.

On the very first day of shoot, I felt at ease working with her because of her friendly attitude and jovial nature. She was always ready to hear my suggestions so I never felt the pressure of working. Even though she was making a serious drama, after she would narrate the scene to me she would be cheerful and happy and find a reason to make everyone laugh and enjoy work.

Tanuja gels with everyone, be it a child, a teenager, a youth or a senior citizen. She transforms herself to be on their level and maturity and can speak to them like a friend. She has a wide range not only in terms of the kind of stories she tells but also on a personal relationship level. She will see things through by hook or by crook, using laughter, friendship and genuine sincere affection. Tanuja is a good director and a good human being. I am happy to know her and work with her.

PRABHU DEVA

'Very often I see the visuals of choreography in my dreams. I get up in the middle of the night and perform the dream steps in my bedroom, so that I don't forget them.'

FILMOGRAPHY

Nuvvostanante Nenoddantana (2005); *Pournami* (2006); *Pokkiri* (2007); *Shankar Dada Zindabad* (2007); *Villu* (2009); *Wanted* (2009); *Engeyum Kadhal* (2011); *Vedi* (2011); *Rowdy Rathore* (2012); *Ramaiya Vastavaiya* (2013); *R . . . Rajkumar* (2013); *Action Jackson* (2014); *Singh Is Bliing* (2015)

SNEAK PEEK

Prabhu Deva was born in Chennai and spent his childhood at Mylapore and Alwarpet. He began his career as a background dancer and assistant choreographer. He became assistant choreographer to his father, M. Sundaram, when he was fourteen years old. He first appeared as a dancer in *Mouna Ragam* (1986), in the song, *'Pani Vizhum'*; his first film as a choreographer was *Vetri Vizha* (1989); he first starred as an actor in *Indhu* (1994); his first film as a director was *Nuvvostanante Nenoddantana* (2005).

MY TAKE

I first met Prabhu Deva while he was shooting *Rowdy Rathore*. He
told me he didn't like talking about himself or his films. I asked
him to trust me on this, the same way he trusts his directors when
he works as an actor or choreographer; he instantly agreed to meet
me for this conversation.

I must mention here, I have not seen some of his regional
films as a choreographer or actor. However, I have loved his work
as a choreographer in *Bombay* (1995), *Pukar* (2000), *Lakshya*
(2004), *Sivaji* (2007), *Wanted*, and some others.

When I interviewed him, he was acting in Remo D'Souza's
film, *ABCD* (2013), and asked me if I could interview him on
location, during the breaks between his shots. He suggested an
audio interview in his vanity van. I agreed because he was so
accommodating. Actors can be very temperamental when they
are shooting, but he was so soft-spoken when I met him on the
sets of *Rowdy Rathore*, which made me feel that he must be calm
while acting.

I had taken along with me a packet of chikki (a snack made
from jaggery and peanuts), because sometimes my blood sugar
level plummets if I skip meals. When this happens, I like to have
something on me instead of the host offering me food.

Just when I began asking him questions, he noticed the packet
and excitedly asked if he could have some. He had the same
twinkle in his eyes as I did whenever I'd see my favourite ice cream,
Chocobar, in my childhood. I was equally delighted by the fact that
the 'Prabhu Deva' had asked me to share my snack with him.

Throughout our conversation—which lasted only for four days,
because he could spare little time between shooting for another
director—I witnessed he was a child with the energy of more than
one adult, a child with an enthusiasm in his work of more than
many professionals. His positive energy was so infectious that every
day I found myself returning home happier. He shared his meals
with me during lunch as if I were a family member. After the

interview, when I would text him my queries, he would often call back and even offer any additional information I needed.

In fact, many months after his interview, he called one morning out of the blue just to ask how I am—that's how affectionate he is. Humble, simple, frank. And kind.

I will always fondly remember how every time I texted him after long intervals, he asked, 'How r u, g? (How are you, sir?) When I gifted him a copy of the first volume of *Directors' Diaries*, he happily agreed to take a selfie and even volunteered to tweet about the book. Thank you, sir. When I left his house that day, I wish I had taken sweet chikki for him, as he had loved it.

THE CONVERSATION

Rakesh Bakshi: *Where were you born? And where did you spend your childhood?*

Prabhu Deva (PD): I was born in Chennai. Till Class VI, I stayed in Mylapore, thereafter my family shifted to Alwarpet as my father bought a house there.

Before we went to school, my mother would make dosas and idlis for us—Raju, my elder brother, Nagendra Prasad, my younger brother, and I. She would sit with us while we ate; I would eat around sixteen dosas or seventeen idlis! In fact, my brothers and I would compete with each other over how many dosas and idlis we could eat in one meal!

I had a normal middle-class life. My parents ensured that my siblings and I had a happy childhood. I think that reflects in my work, for example, in *Nuvvostanante Nenoddantana*, my male lead, Siddharth, is a bubbly, energetic, happy character.

Did you write poems or stories as a child?

PD: My handwriting was very bad and I did not like to write much! Reading and writing were only during school hours, never at home. I was only interested in playing, eating dosas and idlis and sleeping.

Did you attend college after school?

PD: I could not even pass Class XI, so pursuing higher studies was out of the question! But I still remember, after Class IV, I always used to sit alone.

What was your father's profession? Did it influence your career choice?

PD: M. Sundaram, my father, has choreographed about a thousand films. When I was in Class VI or VII, I realized his profession was dancing, because many rehearsals would be held in our house. However, at that time, when he would have rehearsals, I did not like to watch them.

My father forced me to learn Bharatanatyam when I was in Class VII. I did not want to learn the dance form as it was very difficult. The teachers would come home at 6.30 a.m., much before school, so I would get tired. I had to wake up very early to dance and then get ready for school. Eventually, two teachers taught us brothers dance. Dharam Raj Master and Udipi Laxminarayan Master. From Class VII to IX, my teacher was Dharam Raj Master. For the next two years after that, it was Udipi Laxminarayan Master. Because our parents had made it compulsory for us to dance, we did not enjoy it. But, I learnt it with sincerity and never disobeyed our dance masters.

Did you watch a lot of cinema as a child?

PD: My mother used to take us to watch films. The excitement began a day earlier. We always reached the cinema hall an hour early and waited impatiently for the screen to come alive. We didn't go often to watch movies, so those trips were as special to me as the festival of Diwali. The stunts in the action films were what I liked the most.

Who was your emotional anchor, your mother or father?

PD: I cannot live without my mother. When I was in school, at 3.45 p.m. our school bell would ring, and the public transport bus would be waiting outside the gates to ferry us home. I would run the fastest to make sure I didn't miss the bus, so eager I would be to be reunited with my mother.

As a child did you have any specific dream or ambition?

PD: When I was around seven years old, I wanted to join the military, only because I wanted a gun to shoot everyone with!

I joined the film industry when I was fourteen years old after flunking Class XI. I knew I could not have done anything else other than becoming a peon in some office because of my poor qualifications. I began as an assistant choreographer to my father and worked initially as a background dancer. Within the next two years, I became an independent choreographer. I think that is when I decided to be the best dancer, not only in Tamil Nadu but in the whole country! I wanted to give my 100 per cent and worked very hard towards it.

In fact, when I was in Class IX, I had decided that I should always think big and work very hard towards my goals. When I learnt dancing there were no air conditioners or wooden floors, and yet, I rehearsed. Even now, with success behind me, I do not seek a comfort zone during rehearsals. I just work, whatever the circumstances may be.

Even though I have a successful career, I have never owned a professional music system. When my producers or directors give me the audio CD of the song I've to choreograph, I play it on my regular DVD player. Or I use my car's music system to listen to the song while travelling.

When did you realize that there is a profession called the 'director'?

PD: I knew about it before I became an independent choreographer, while assisting my father. I never wanted to be a director back then. I loved playing cricket and even after becoming an independent choreographer, I sought opportunities to play. I always kept a bat, ball and stumps on the film set to play cricket during breaks. Even now, if there is a ground nearby and I have a break, I love playing cricket with my crew.

While choreographing or watching a film, did you observe any director and think, 'This is a good director and I want to be like them someday'?

PD: Never. When I am choreographing, I only think about the song. I always think that my work, whatever I am doing at the moment, has to be the best. I am very focused. I have never been distracted by anything or anyone else. If I had thought of other things while choreographing, like wanting to be an actor or director, I would not have achieved anything in life. For me, choreography is more than being focused, more than a passion; it is an obsession, a madness. Whenever I receive the audio of the song I have to choreograph, I get so excited, so eager, so passionate to do my best that I end up not sleeping that night.

Very often I see the visuals of choreography in my dreams. I get up in the middle of the night and perform the dream steps in my bedroom, so that I don't forget them. Only after perfecting the steps do I go back to sleep. This has happened innumerable times, ever since I was sixteen years old. The next morning I go for rehearsal and perform the same steps for the actors and dancers.

Was your first job as a choreographer or a dancer?

PD: It must have been around 1986 and I was probably ten or eleven years old at the time, when I went to meet my father in Ooty, during the outdoor shoot of a song he was choreographing. It was a film directed by Mani Ratnam, *Mouna Ragam*. My father introduced me to Mani Sir, saying, I was learning Bharatanatyam. He then played a song from a cassette player and told me to perform what I had learnt so far. Had my mother been present, I would've said no, but my father was there and I knew I couldn't say no to him. Because even if I had said no, my father would've insisted, and I would've had to obey him. I wanted to get done with it and leave as soon as possible.

I performed for about four minutes. After my performance, Mani Sir suggested I dance to a shot in the film where a tune was being played on a flute. I did it and was paid Rs 500 for my performance. That was my first income, for a special appearance in the song '*Pani Vizhum*'.

Which was your first job as an independent choreographer?

PD: It was a song for *Vetri Vizha*, a Tamil film, with Kamal Hassan sir. The title means, 'celebration of success'. My father was the chief choreographer, but he was not available as he was working on the next set. The producer told him if he was busy, he could send me as I was his assistant. My father said, 'Yes, take Prabhu Deva, he will do the song.' The producer was confident I could do it. But I was tense when I heard about it. It was a very big responsibility, especially considering it were Kamal Hassan sir and Sivaji Productions. I was nervous because my father was not going to be present. But thankfully, I got enough time to prepare for it.

When I listen to the song I have to choreograph, I go into my own world. From somewhere, the strength just comes; it is God's blessing, I know.

Which was your first film as a director?

PD: It was a Telugu film called *Nuvvostanante Nenoddantana*. The title translates to, 'If You Say You Are Arriving, I Will Not Say No.' The film is like a poem, a love story; it's a fun film.

Who was the producer of your first film and how did you meet him?

PD: M.S. Raju. I knew him because I had choreographed for him when I was seventeen. After I became an actor, I choreographed a song for a film he was producing, which became a big hit. The song was, '*Varsham*', in which the heroine danced in the rain. It was during that time that he asked me if I would like to direct a film for him. Five years before his offer, I had decided I wanted to direct a film. So I immediately answered yes. I really wanted to experience something new through direction. I am grateful to him for giving me my first opportunity to direct.

What was that 'new' experience?

PD: A director has the unique ability to transform words into images. He is the captain of a film and it is his vision that the audience sees on the silver screen. It is this experience that I was seeking. However, in this profession, you can be brilliant and yet not be able to make a film because it is really hard to find the right people and have all the elements in the right place for your dream to become reality.

How can a director help a producer in controlling the budget of his or her film?

PD: By being empathetic! By thinking of the producer's investment before their creativity; it is as simple as that!

As an actor, what do you look for in a script or a director?

PD: I first consider the team behind the script and then the script. By team, I mean I like to know who the producer, writer and director are. If I am satisfied with them, only then do I ask for the script.

'You can be a director one day,' did this come from within or did someone tell you this?

PD: I heard it myself, very clearly, otherwise, I could not have been a director. But I heard it only after I became an actor. When I would get a scene to act, I would think of the other ways it could be directed or even performed. Direction is all about willingly taking on challenges, responsibilities, stress, loving them and asking for more! I feel nervous and anxious while directing a movie but those feelings make me more productive and creative.

What aspects of a director's job make it stressful and challenging?

PD: Maintaining the crew, technicians, actors, script, taking the final call on any and every question. Life's about challenges and a film director's job is very challenging. They have no rest. However, in spite of the stress and responsibilities, it is a fun profession. Whatever you want, you, the director, can create. When I am directing big stars, I do feel tense before the shoot. However, it vanishes when I am shooting with them because then, I am in the moment and confident.

When you direct, do you ever do rehearsals or readings with your actors?

PD: No. I believe in spontaneity. And, I believe, spontaneity is lost when the script is rehearsed by the actors before the shoot.

What are actors looking for in a new director when they agree to work with them?

PD: Big actors have worked with many directors, big and small. If a new director has been assisting any big director, the actor would have noticed their work and known if they have the potential to direct a film all on their own. Sometimes actors believe what the producer believes, so if a producer is backing a new director, they agree to work with them too. Sometimes the new director is the son or daughter of an established producer or director, which enables them to get a break faster. However, if you are well-connected, you may get your first film, but if you are not talented, you will not get your second or third film.

How much do you involve yourself in the other departments of filmmaking?

PD: I go into every detail of every department. I am the director after all, and anyone from any department can ask me a technical question. So I like to prepare in depth. I select the colour of the actor's shoelaces and decide if the heroine will wear nail polish and in which colour. Even without a shot list, I can tell what the second shot or the fifteenth one would be and why numbers eleven or eighteen can only be shot from a particular angle. Everyone in my team prepares thoroughly during preproduction. And everyone is encouraged to offer suggestions or ask questions. So I have to be clear about why I want what I want.

Do you make storyboards for your films?

PD: I do not even write properly, so how can I think of sketching storyboards! If I want to make a storyboard for a song or an action shoot, I will tell a storyboard artist my vision and let him create it. I believe I can express what I need to my technicians easily, so I don't need storyboards.

What is a typical morning like on the day you shoot?

PD: I feel excited and can't wait to reach the set. I keep thinking of the various techniques that I would employ to make the scene more interesting, more dynamic and more fun to watch. Cinema should be fun to watch.

A day before the shoot, my associate director and I discuss the scenes we will be shooting. We brainstorm nuances, mannerisms or some unique behavioural elements we could add to make the character and the scene more interesting.

The next day, I narrate how I see the shots, one after the other, and that's when my direction assistants prepare the shot division for the scene. We do this for all the scenes we are going to shoot that day.

Why is music and dance so important to us in Indian films?

PD: It is in our culture. I do not know about Mumbai, but in Tamil Nadu when a child is born, the occasion is celebrated with music and dance. During the life of a person, many significant occasions are celebrated with dance and music. When a person dies, in many communities the mourners accompany the body to the crematorium or burial site with music and dance. Right from our birth to our death, music and dance remain integral parts of our lives.

When some people question me, 'From where have fifty dancers appeared in the song?' I say, 'Let them earn their bread; why are you asking so many questions that will not help them fill their stomachs or feed their families? Why question the livelihood of these poor, sincere, talented people?' In addition, song and dance scenes are entertaining. And I make films to entertain, so I believe in them.

What does cinema mean to a common person?

PD: Cinema is a fantastical dream for a common person! What he cannot possibly achieve, he comes to see and experience it on the silver screen and feel happy. The common man comes to the cinema hall to be entertained. In fact, even I don't go for a movie to ask questions but to have good time.

Considering you began as a choreographer, did you choreograph the songs of your first film as director?

PD: Vishnu choreographed my first film as a director. Since I was the director, I did not want to be the choreographer too. In this respect, I believe, two brains are better than one. I never think I am the best or that I must do everything myself just because I have some other skill too.

If I choreograph and direct my film to 'show-off' how I am great at multitasking, it would be very tiring and monotonous. By taking on someone else with talents/skills different from my own, a new style can emerge in my film, something that is different and maybe even better than what I have ever done before. This can only happen when you allow other talents to add and contribute to your own work. Why should it always just be my style of dance?

Moreover, with someone else choreographing my songs, there will be less tension for me as the director. He will do his job of choreographing, while I will do mine of directing and we will both end up doing much better jobs. By not choreographing the songs myself, I will also have an objective view, an outside view, of the choreography, which I will not get if I choreograph and direct.

Further, when I choreograph, I am a very different person. I do not want that person to interfere with the director in me. As a choreographer, people think I am a demon and that is because I am unwilling to compromise and would do anything to get what I want. But even as a director, I do not compromise and do everything to get what I want. I will end up fighting with myself if I direct and choreograph. If I allow someone else to choreograph, there will still be a difference between me as a choreographer and me as a director.

I treat the relationship of a choreographer and a director like that of a father and sons, the director being the father and the choreographer, the son. The son can throw tantrums and have his way. But the father, the director, cannot. That for me is a necessary compromise that a director makes.

Another perspective being, when I am choreographing, my work lasts for just three–four days. But when I am the director, my work lasts for sixty or ninety days. So I cannot be rude to anyone. If I am rude, everybody will get disturbed and my film will suffer. So as a director I compromise on my temper too, just so that everything goes smoothly. When I am directing I tell actors, do not get stressed out. Give all your stress to me. I will take care of them for you. So, basically, as a director, I compromise on my own feelings to make everyone around me feel comfortable.

Who was the editor of your first film?

PD: Krishna Reddy. He was already editing a film for my producer and I decided to use him for my film too. There was no need for me to make choices. The best technicians were available to me, but more than me, they had to decide whether they wanted to work with me. After all, it was I who was the first-time director; they were all established in their fields!

During editing, my associate director lines up the scenes for me to view. After viewing their suggestions, I make Reddy edit them the way I envisioned them. Often, I shoot in a manner that the material is almost edit-ready. Also, I never shoot additional angles, extra set-ups, or take unnecessary coverage to make it easier for the editor to know my point of view. It also saves the producer's money. I think I can do that because of my experience as a choreographer and an actor. That has helped me a lot.

Do you think because you were an actor, it is easier for you to get big stars to act for you? In the sense, they trust you more because they know you are an actor?

PD: I think, because I am an actor, I can understand them much better. I can understand their timing, moods and doubts. They are free to ask me, tell me anything they want and I will take it upon myself to reply and provide them with a comfort zone. I explain the character to them in detail and sometimes show them by performing the scene the way I see it. Then I tell them to give it to me in their own way, from their point of view.

Is it a director's job to also manage people's egos?

PD: Who does not have an ego? If you are a successful director, people don't get egotistical around you, they listen to you. But if you're not, everyone will try to have their way with you. You have to understand these aspects and create a balance somehow.

As a first-time director, how did you deal with solicited or unsolicited suggestions?

PD: During preproduction, I received a lot of suggestions from my team, but not on the set. I ask for suggestions and tell them if I agree to their suggestions, I will use them in the film. But like I mentioned before, we all dive into the detailing of the script during preproduction and production. For example, if we are shooting on the sixtieth day of a film that will take seventy-five days to shoot and I receive a suggestion on the set that I do not agree with it, I explain to the giver why I am rejecting it. I study the script so well that I can counter any suggestion with good reasoning. 'What we shot in that particular schedule, scene number so and so, will not allow us to accept your suggestion now.'

I am not saying this because I am overconfident about my abilities, but because we all work very hard on the scripting process. When we sit to script, although I do not understand Hindi much, I do understand what is being said from the way the words sound. Even now, during the making of my next film, *Rowdy Rathod*, when Shiraz, my writer, narrates what he has written, I can say it goes with my character and scene just from the way the words sound to me. I can even pinpoint unnecessary words being used in a scene, in a dialogue, just from the way the sentence sounds to me and its timing. There should be no extra dialogue, because it ruins the flow, the pace and the timing of the dialogue and the scene. Very often, we argue about our differing opinions, but something good always comes out of these creative fights. While shooting *Rowdy Rathod*, my actors gave us suggestions and I accepted them. They are experienced actors, so I paused to consider their suggestions.

Some directors like to stand next to the camera and direct and some sit by the video-assist monitor and direct, what is your usual method?

PD: When the actors are performing emotional scenes, I stand next to the camera. I want to be right next to the camera, so that when they perform, I can convey the expression and the response they are seeking from me. I never look through the camera viewfinder, even during rehearsals. Only when the cinematographer suggests that I should view the rehearsal through the viewfinder, I do so.

Who was your music composer? And, because you were a choreographer, did you feel there was pressure on you to create some extraordinary choreography in your first film?

PD: Devi Shree Prasad was my music composer. He is very good. He must have been about twenty-six or twenty-seven back then. I think, my producer chose me to direct the film because he believed I had the potential to do it and not just direct the songs. So I never felt any pressure to do any extraordinary choreography to prove something to someone, and even my script did not need it. There were six songs, of which only two were with dances. One was a fantasy song and the other five were woven into the screenplay. Four of the songs showed the progression of the story through montages. The fantasy one was the climax song and it did not require much choreography.

I was true to the script and did what the script demanded and not what the choreographer in me wanted. A director has to be true only to his script, whatever be his other skills or talents.

How did you feel when you saw your first rushes and dailies?

PD: Confident, I think. Everybody said the rushes were good and I agreed. I felt that the video-assist monitor is a big minus point for me. Because of the monitor, I have already seen the video images of what we are shooting so when I view the dailies or rushes during the editing process, I do not feel the impact of viewing the moving images for the first time. If you want to judge the rushes and dailies, do not view the shooting on the video-assist monitor. Otherwise, the fun of seeing the images for the first time during edit is lost!

What is your process with your core team after you finalize the script?

PD: Once the script is finalized, I sit with assistant directors and my associate director, and we identify the most important scenes from the script. We take up one scene at a time and discuss it in absolute detail. We evaluate each and every idea that anybody in our team comes up with, and all team members have complete freedom to say what they want to, provide any number of ideas or criticism on how the scene can be better. When ideas are given, we all openly discuss why the new idea will work or why it will not. Once we have decided which new ideas and suggestions work, we shortlist them and give them to the writer to incorporate them in his next draft of the scene. Then the writer and I work on the rewrite of the scenes already discussed and add the new ideas that the team has finalized.

Once the writer is ready with the rewrite, I get together with my team for the second time to discuss the dialogues. This time we only discuss any new ideas emerging on the dialogue front.

Once we decide what new ideas can work for improving the dialogues, the writer is instructed to do the next rewrite, but only for the dialogues. This is the process I follow to evolve the scenes till the shooting stage.

Just before the shooting schedule arrives, we identify all those scenes that are going to be shot in the next schedule. During this third session of brainstorming, the team discussing the scenes is smaller. Only the core direction team, such as the first assistant director and my writer, is part of the third session. I involve the cinematographer and the art director only four or five days before the schedule. I give them a full narration of the scenes to be shot in the schedule and discuss everything they need for their work. I tell them where it is happening, why, when, the background required, day or night, anything and everything they need to know to do their job well. I follow the same procedure for the art director, costume designer and production designer. My cinematographer will know all that is happening. I do not disclose too much detail to the costume designer and others.

You were a choreographer first, then an actor, and now a director. Is choreography, acting, direction, a journey for you or destination?

PD: Journey. However, a 'journey' did not make me a choreographer. I became a choreographer only because I was a school dropout. I had no other career option. When I was choreographing, I did not want to be an actor and I did not know that I would become one someday. Acting happened naturally during the process of choreography. It's only when I became an actor that I realized I can be a director or at least I became ambitious enough to want to be a director someday, but I did not know whether it would ever happen.

My journey as a choreographer made me an actor. And my journey as an actor helped me discover direction. Yet, I don't see myself as a choreographer, actor or director. I see myself as a person who simply wants to entertain people. Whether I am a choreographer, actor or director, or whether I am sad or happy or depressed, I just want the audience to enjoy my films. I want them to be happy when they see my films. I do not believe in giving any messages in my films. You don't need to make a film to give a message. Even the producer expects me to entertain the audience, and if people enjoy the film, it will help the producer earn back his investment.

Every time I watched a film as a child, I felt as happy as though it was the joyful festival of Diwali. Therefore, I want my audience to enjoy my films as well. If they see my film or me, I want them to feel a happy energy. That is why my action and my dances are fast, high-paced. I just want to transfer my positive energy to my audience. I've never wanted anything more from my life in cinema.

Someday when your child grows up and tells you he/she wants to be a film-maker, what will you advise as a parent?

PD: In the future, if my children come and tell me what they want to be, it will be a very big thing for me. I will be happy that at least they are telling me or asking my permission or advice. Because I don't expect that from the next generation. And if I am given that much respect, it will indeed be very nice. Any parent will want their child to be happy and in a good position in their life and career. After all, we are all earning for their future happiness.

I will be very happy if my children ask me for my advice. But I will tell them, 'Do not take advice from me or anyone. Do what you want to do with your life.' If you ask me to give them a specific advice, like, joining a film school or making a short film or becoming an assistant director, I won't do that. My father did not give me any advice and I did not ask him for any. He simply told me, 'What you want to do with your life, you must do.' And then he supported me in all my decisions. In the same way, I will support my children in any decision they take.

Would you like to share something from your experiences so far with today's generation?

PD: Wherever you may be, be happy. Whatever you do, do happily. Whatever your situation or circumstances may be, try to be happy. That is it! We all have happiness and it is inside us. Do not look for it outside. It is very difficult to find happiness like that. Happiness can be found in the simplest of acts and things around you. As simple as this packet of jaggery chikki you have brought along for us to have after lunch. Just the thought of having it makes me feel happy! And when I will have it, I will feel even happier.

For me, happiness lies in the small things. I would say, do not lose the value of the small things because they can bring us bigger happiness. If going for a film makes you happy, go for it. Even when I get a new shirt, I am very happy. The brand does not matter. The fact that I am going to wear a new shirt excites me! So I actually plan the special moment when I will wear the new shirt. For me, any new shirt is a very good shirt, irrespective of its cost. Even the planning and decision of when I will wear it, makes me happy.

I say, be happy with simple things like chocolates, ice cream, normal clothes, festivals, watching a film. Get excited by the smallest things just like you did when you were a child. I never forget the happiness I had as a child.

If you gave me the DVD of a film to watch, I will feel very happy that today I will get to watch a film after work. It's exactly how happy I felt when my Mother would take us to the cinema hall and we would wait in the empty hall to view the film. As happy as when Diwali would come, we would burst crackers and hide our crackers from each other. That was happiness. I would steal my brother's share of Diwali crackers and burn them! My mother would make sweets for Diwali and Pongal. When my mother would be busy talking to guests, we would sneak into the kitchen and eat the sweets she had prepared or I would steal a packet of sweets and run off to eat them! That was pure happiness.

Now, whenever I choreograph, they are as happy moments as having those sweets my mother made or when I burst crackers as a child. As a director, I feel thrilled each and every day on set or location. I am as happy as I was as a child when I choreograph and even when I direct.

I say all this because my advice is: Do not lose the sight of the smallest things that can make you happy. The big ones will automatically bring you happiness too. That is my pursuit through my work and life. Be as happy as when you were a child.

You believe, 'I make films only because I want people to be happy watching my films,' and your advice to the younger generation would be, 'Be Happy.'

PD: I truly believe that. The only education, talent and skill I have is dance. With dance what else can I possibly do for society or people other than entertain? I am not a doctor that I can serve the needy and help people. Dance has the capacity to entertain and entertainment spreads happiness. That's the very best I can do for people with whatever little God has gifted me. Dance brought happiness to my heart and that's what I want to pass on to the next generation—happiness.

PERSPECTIVE FROM ANOTHER LENS

Cinematographer Kiran Deohans speaks of Prabhu Deva

I have done one film with Prabhu Deva, *Ramaiya Vastavaiya*. He had seen some of my earlier films and felt I could give the 'gloss' he required for this one. He told me *Ramaiya Vastavaiya* is about love and passion. If there is something that marked my work on this film, it was the easiness, the simplicity, of the story, because I had to resort to basic, organic images to convey the earthiness Prabhu Deva wanted.

I had a lot of elbow space, working with him; although he is very sure of what he wants, yet he gives immense creative liberty to his DOP. For example, we had readied an elaborate set for the very first schedule of the film. Once it was completed, the producer, Kumar Taurani-ji, thought it would make sense if an additional song were shot on the same set. I was game. Accordingly, they showed me a visual reference of the kind of feel they required for the song. However, on seeing it, I felt it would be wrong to shoot the song on the existing set, as it was architecturally very different from the 'look and feel' they wanted. Anyway, I had to shoot the song, so shooting here or elsewhere would make no difference to me; however, to stay true to the film I communicated my apprehension and suggestions to Prabhu Deva. He immediately understood and convinced the producer that it made more sense to construct a new set for the song they had to shoot. He displayed great faith in me and even went that extra mile.

Simplicity and clarity, these are the two keywords that describe Prabhu Deva—simplicity of thought and clarity of mind. There is simplicity in the way he takes his shots, in his narrative; there are no complex symbols or motifs. He does not attempt to intellectualize the shot or narrative. The grammar of his film is crystal clear.

Another thing I like about him is his ability to listen to reason. If at times I felt that maybe a certain lens was preferable to another, he would want to understand why, and if my reasoning made sense to him, he would always agree. Of course, there were times he would still insist on the lensing he wants, and that's absolutely correct because finally, he is the director and we are all following his vision. And what's great about him is that he will appreciate a suggestion and will make it a point to tell me later he liked it.

Prabhu Deva is the king of improvisation. He's an awesome choreographer, so his sense of timing is excellent. Even after a scene is lit and ready for take, he will suggest a change in the camera angle and ask if it were okay to tweak it a bit. So his mind is always working, always improvising. Once I understood that about him, I kept myself alert for that eventuality always, so that I could quickly deliver the changes he required.

Being a 100 per cent professional himself, he does not have the patience to tolerate mediocrity and incompetency. He is capable of losing his temper, but that is a positive thing because that push is necessary to deliver good work. He is disciplined and that extends to simple things, like, breaking for meals on time. It is important because the entire unit works on tight discipline then. And he is so fast; it's amazing. The amount of work he can finish in a shift without sacrificing quality, without compromising on any creativity, must be applauded.

On a personal level, he is a fantastic human being at heart. And what I like about him is that if he reacts to you in a certain manner, that behaviour is constant. Whether you are on set or at a social event, his behaviour towards you will not change. He may come across as a no-nonsense and tough person, but he is actually very sensitive and nice. I have thoroughly enjoyed working with him.

SPOTLIGHT ON

SPOT BOY SALIM SHAIKH
(ACTION)

Rakesh Bakshi: *How did you come to be known as 'Action'?*

Salim Shaikh (SS): Director Prakash Mehra-ji would address me as 'Action'. Once on a film shoot, back in the 1980s, he asked me to get water for him, and I got it quickly. He told me, 'You get me the tobacco every time I ask for it faster than my seasoned actors begin their performance when I shout "Action"! From now onwards, I will address you as Action, and I hope it will motivate my actors to be as quick as you!' I laughed and went about my work, but over the years this name stuck and now even those I have worked with for over three decades do not know that my real name is Salim.

Do film crews usually call you by your name or address you as 'Spot Dada'?

SS: Few people address us by our names. We like it when they address as a Spot Dada, but it feels great when we know that they know our names. We spot boys do many odd jobs in the long chain of film-making and are largely unnoticed and sometimes appreciated by the crew. People who watch films are unaware of our work and our significance on the film set. Even the people who handle lights and the settings department have greater visibility than us.

There was a time we spot boys would travel from person to person on the film set and offer them water. Nowadays, we just stash a bucket with bottled water and keep it outside the shooting floor and the crew helps itself. We used to hold three glasses in one hand, a kettle of hot tea in the other and do the rounds of the set every now and then until pack-up. We would get skin rashes and burns from the hot kettle; I still have those marks. There was a Punjabi cook who used to make tea in Tony Juneja sir's films; he would remove the milk cream aside in a bowl while making tea for the crew and very kindly give it to us spot boys to use as medicine for our burns and rashes.

Tell us about your formative years.

SS: I must be around 60–61 years old and from Rajasthan. I have never been to school because I couldn't afford to; also, I wasn't interested. My father was a goatherd. We had 400–500 goats and we used to sell wool. When there was a wedding in the village and they played loud music, and after everyone in my house had fallen sleep, I used to sneak out to listen to the songs and come back only around 5 in the morning. This built my interest in music. Some of my friends and I were very mischievous and were always up to something, be it bathing in the lake at night or eating corn or cucumber from other's farms. Back in those days, the ceramists used to have donkeys and we used to cut the rope with which they were tied with a sharp stone and sit on them and ride around. In the morning we used to get caught and were beaten by our parents.

I ran away from home because I did not want to be a goatherd. I went to Didwana, Rajasthan, and worked at a tea stall for about nine months, never wanting to go back home. I washed utensils. Then I travelled to Jaipur and tried looking for jobs in the hotels there, but couldn't find any. During that time, director Raj Kumar Kohli sir had come to Jaipur to shoot his film.

Who are the people who may have helped you reach here and become a spot boy?

SS: A man named Kapoor once saw me hanging around idly and sought my help to carry vegetables that he had purchased for the crew's meal from the market to the kitchen at the shooting location. I helped him and then started doing odd jobs in the kitchen. Thereafter, he made me his permanent assistant.

Witnessing the film shoot, I made up my mind that I wanted to work with them and wanted to go to Bombay after the shooting got over in Jaipur. I met the unit supervisor. He treated me well and like a kid. He advised me that there was no permanency in the film line if I worked as a spot boy. Sometimes there would be work and sometimes nothing for months or even a year. But I insisted and requested him to take me with them to Bombay. But he didn't, as there was no space in the bus.

I had saved Rs 1500 from the odd jobs I had done after running away from home. When I came to Bombay, I was robbed of my money at Dadar railway station and became penniless. The conductor of the public bus I was travelling in was very kind and took pity on me and took me to his house at Worli that night. He gave me dinner and the next day he gave me breakfast too. This was sometime in the 1980s. He even gave me Rs 100 to spend on travel and food. I had to travel to Khar Danda [Khar West] to look for someone who was going to help me find a job in the film industry. At Khar Danda, I happened to meet Mathur Bhai, the film unit's cook and he allowed me to stay with him for a few days. He was a very good man. However, I did not find work in Bombay so I returned to Jaipur.

Mathur Bhai returned to Jaipur for another shoot so I met him. He had come to shoot Raj Kumar Kohli's film. I did odd jobs on that shoot for the crew. When the shooting schedule was over, I asked Mathur Bhai to take me to Bombay with him so I could work as a spot boy in the films. He agreed.

Tell us about some of the directors you loved working with.

SS: I miss working with Raj Kumar Kohli sir. He had a good nature and respected everyone, including spot boys and light men. I have seen many directors wasting their producers' money during shoots by being lazy and uncertain. They are not focused. Raj Kumar Kohli sir never wasted time. Nowadays, I like working with directors Anil Sharma sir, Raj Kanwar sir, and Aanand L. Rai sir, who reminds me of the directors of the olden days because of his good nature. I have done three films with him. He is so humble and down to earth. If any spot boy, light men or anyone is having food and he likes something on their plate, he will ask them for a bite and pick it up and eat it. In the morning when he comes on set, he shakes hands with everybody, including us. A cinematographer I love to work with is Anil Mehta. I also like working with line producer Shashikant Sinha.

How keenly do you observe the process of film-making and the crew on set?

SS: I may be just a spot boy, but we can tell in a few minutes if a director knows their job or if they are making a fool of their unit. We have worked with so many of them. I can even tell a good actor in a few shots. I think a good director is like the head of the family or the captain of a team. They make sure that everyone works together like a team. According to me, director Jahnu Barua has these qualities. I have done only one film with him, *Har Pal* (2005). We had gone to Shillong for the shoot. Before the shoot he would sit with all of us and explain to us what had to be shot that day.

It's also important that a director should not litter, spit here or there and respect the women working on the film. A hit film doesn't automatically mean that its director is a good person.

Actor Shashi Kapoor sir was one of my favourites. He would get chhole bhature for all the spot boys, production people, light men, etc. He was a foodie and shared his delights with us. He used to get tandoori mutton and place it on the table and whoever wanted to eat was welcome to help themselves. He never discriminated. There is another person in this industry whom I respect a lot because he respects our work, production designer and art director Nitin Desai. And a cameraman whom I admire a lot is Anil Mehta. He cares for his light men and spot boys.

How important are you really to the film-making process? Would it be justified if I address you too as a film-maker?

SS: According to me, spot boys, light men and the settings department lay the foundation every day in film-making. These three departments together help the unit set up a shoot every day and clear things post pack-up, when all the technicians, actors, cinematographer, producer, director, have gone home. We stay around for at least two more hours after everyone has left and arrive an hour or two before the others. Yet, we are paid only for the duration of our fixed shifts and never for overtime.

How have you managed to maintain your family while working in a profession some would consider insecure?

SS: I have two sons, both of whom are in school, and I have kept them away from the film line because I feel politics and our film industry today are the same. Because of too much competition, many of us get exploited. My family has, over the decades, sometimes not had adequate meals because we work only when the shooting starts, so my wife and children have seen some challenging days. However, I was honoured a few years ago, in 2016–17, by the audience and guests—music composer Pyarelal-ji [Laxmikant-Pyarelal]; Rakesh Bakshi, son of noted lyricist Anand Bakshi; and director Ketan Desai, son of director Manmohan Desai—during a screening of *Amar Akbar Anthony* (1977), thanks to Radio Nasha, for having worked on this film as a spot boy back in the 1970s. That night on the way back home, my wife said, 'I sometimes think my husband is in a wastrel profession, insecure and one that does not pay adequately, however, seeing him being honoured by people connected with the film world and those who contributed to this film he had once worked on made me feel very proud of him. And his teary eyes and big smile at that moment made me forget all those difficult years that we have endured.'

The profession of spot boys is not just unreliable, because we are hired only when a film rolls, but also because we are not paid adequately. Over the years, a lot of people advised me to do something else for a livelihood, but I always held myself back in fear that I was not educated and thinking that at least being a spot boy fed my family. I drive an autorickshaw between films to meet our family's expenses. I don't know how I have lasted here.

Maybe, there are three things because of which I am still there in this industry: (1) my honesty (2) my good behaviour and good relations with people I have worked with, and many really fine producers and directors who helped me give them my best; and (3) I have no ego. These three virtues matter a lot in this profession. Some people may perceive us spot boys to be on the bottom rung of the ladder, yet, we are people the crew must be able to count on. I hope I have done justice to the films and people I have worked with over the decades.

MAKE-UP DESIGNER
VIKRAM GAIKWAD

Rakesh Bakshi: *Do you have a memory of your first realization of what 'make-up' meant? And how did you get your first break in cinema?*

Vikram Gaikwad (VG): I was eight or nine years old, living in Pune, and working in a children's drama, when I discovered an inherent fascination for make-up rooms, which were full of masks and colourful costumes. Babanrao Shinde was the make-up artist and he supplied costumes and make-up to theatre groups. In one of the plays, I witnessed two children, nearly my age, being transformed—one into a skeleton and the other into a witch—with make-up and costumes. When these two child actors appeared in front of the audience, everyone got scared. Because I had witnessed their transformation, I wasn't scared. I was fascinated by the power of make-up. By the time I reached Class VII, I was sure I had found my true calling and devoted myself to it, thereby quitting studies after Class XII and assisting my guru, Babanrao Shinde, full time.

My next big break in this profession came when legendary make-up artist Anji Babu, from FTII, needed an assistant, because of his excessive workload. Thanks to Anji Babu I learnt most of what I know today from my four years with him at FTII. He was my second guru.

The person who motivated me tremendously was the head of the art direction department at FTII, Mahesh Tawre. Mahesh-ji saw immense talent in me and insisted I leave FTII and travel to Bombay to work in films. And I did.

My first break in films came when director Shyam [Benegal] Babu saw the make-up I had done on a young man, transforming him into the legendary Khan Abdul Ghaffar Khan. Shyam Babu was producing a biopic then, *Sardar* (1993), on the life of Sardar Vallabhbhai Patel. After that film, Shyam Babu took me to South Africa, for *The Making of the Mahatma* (1996). He told me something I never forgot, 'If you want respect in this profession, demand the script first. If the producer or director does not give you the script, do not work with him.'

What kind of thoughts come to your mind while you are reading the script? And what is your process of working with the director after you have read the script?

VG: While I am reading scripts I get ideas about what it needs. In my subconscious, I have a bank of characters and their nuances, be it visual or physical, and while I am reading, those visuals surface in my mind. I have in my subconscious mind, what can be termed a 'character bank'. After Class XII, while working with my guru, Babanrao Shinde, I'd gone to hundreds of villages where I observed different kinds of skin tones, characters and facial features. Those visuals are alive in me even today. Even today, while I'm sitting here with you, I'm also observing other people around. That is what I do all the time. So when I am reading a script, visuals of people I have seen sometime somewhere appear to me as the faces and physical attributes of the characters in the story. A script is textual, but it's my visual memory that provides me the faces to the names of the characters.

I will then sometimes sketch the characters I have in mind before I meet the director and offer him or her visual references of how I see them. Sometimes, directors offer me visual references and I make a sincere attempt to match their visual references. Often directors know the temperament of their characters but they cannot visualize the face, so I step in to provide that. But most of the time, it is usually my first depiction of the characters that are, invariably, in one form or another, selected.

Anything else you want to share from your experiences that is significant to the art of make-up?

VG: The job of a make-up artist is not only to apply make-up but to also tell directors when it is required and when it is not. Unfortunately, many actors, especially females, and directors do not understand or appreciate this. They force us to apply make-up even when it is not required. For example, if you want a young girl to look like a mature woman, simply apply a lot of make-up. But, if the aim of the story is to retain the innocence and youth of the character, by forcing me to apply too much make-up, the actor or director is going against the essence of the character.

Shyam Babu and Mani Ratnam always like their actors to have a natural look. However, giving them a natural look does not mean I will not use make-up. It means I may create the illusion of making them look 'natural', as if no make-up has been used even when it has, which is a terrific skill that few have.

How would you describe the art of make-up?

VG: Make-up is the craft of illusion. If the audience sees through a magician's tricks, they fail as an illusionist. Same applies to a make-up artist. If the audience appreciates the make-up I've done on an actor, I've failed as a make-up artist. My work has to be invisible. This applies to everything in cinema, all departments' contribution should be invisible for the film to seem believable.

What is the difference between doing make-up on Indians and Caucasians?

VG: White skin without make-up looks kind of pale or fake. So I have to add life to that skin. How do you add life? By blood. Because blood is life. And blood is red. So I add a blood tone colour to their make-up. Most Indian actresses have good skin and need only corrections—basically even out the tone by getting rid of dark circles, pimples and decolourization.

As a make-up artist when you say someone has lovely skin, what do you mean?

VG: I have complimented Nandita Das for her beautiful skin. In *Omkara*, I suggested to the director Vishal Bhardwaj that the actors, especially Kareena, must be shown with nude skin, meaning no make-up. He agreed. So Kareena had no make-up in the film, in spite of her protests. I made her realize how beautiful her skin naturally is. For the blush effect, we would simply rub her cheeks with a soft *malmal* cloth.

What kind of discussions do you usually have with the DOP, the cameraman?

VG: Every DOP has their own style or pattern of lighting. While the artist is being readied in the make-up room or vanity van, I personally visit the set or location and observe the style of lighting being employed by the DOP. Some deploy a straight/direct lighting pattern, some use very strong key-lighting, some are masters in hard, shallow lighting, etc. It's important for me to observe the light that will be falling on the actors. Film stock is very friendly to light, unlike the digital medium. The digital medium is non-friendly to make-up, because it lacks the rich and superior texture of film stock, and thus the image looks inferior in digital compared to film stock. Film stock is more sensitive to light and hence the image looks far superior.

So, I always do the final make-up of an artist in natural light or on the set or location that is already lit for the shoot. That gives me the correct sense of how light will act on the artist's skin. In a way, I blend the make-up to the DOP's lighting style, so they complement each other. The DOPs also know how to use light to cover up flaws or limitations in make-up, and even art direction or performance, if need be. Honestly, I would rather accept the limitations of make-up and seek the help of the DOP than be bull-headed and arrogant and overdo the make-up, thereby making the flaw in the actor's skin more noticeable and worse. Therefore, even if you were to compliment me for any job I have done well, I would humbly like to share credit with the DOP, as we complement each other in creating the correct image that the script deserves.

However, even lighting has its limitations, however brilliant and experienced the DOP might be. Everyone has. And with such an understanding and humility when a director, an art director, a DOP, a make-up artist and a costume designer come together as a team, great work results.

Does it happen, that sometimes when you watch a film you realize that in the DI process the shades you gave the actor/s during make-up changed?

VG: Yes, it happens often. Because we are mostly never consulted during the final stages of post-production or the DI stage. Sometimes I have given an actor a light pink shade in their facial make-up and when I view the film in the cinema hall, the colour has changed to magenta! That change makes the actress look 'sharp', instead of the intended 'soft' or 'innocent' look that the script had mentioned.

Of 100, only twenty directors bother to show us the film while the DI process is on. It's not that the directors do not call us, sometimes it's the DOPs who don't think it's important that we are consulted.

Any difference between men and women actors you have noticed?

VG: Although many people think it must be women who are fussy about their 'looks', it has been my experience that most of them are trusting of their make-up artist. In fact, many male actors want to look at their image before and after each and every take, every ten seconds sometimes! And many male actors tend to use even more make-up then female actors.

What are the challenges that you face when you create FX prosthesis?

VG: FX prosthesis is the process of using prosthetic sculpting, moulding and casting techniques to create advanced cosmetic effects. The craft of prosthetic make-up is a nightmare in India because of the heat and humidity. Prosthetics are usually created by the application of foam pieces or silicon rubber pieces over the skin. For the foam or skin-safe silicone rubber to stick to the skin, we use a 'medical' gum—a paste that is skin-safe. The problem that arises is that the sweat from the heat or humidity dissolves the medical gum, thus weakening the bond between the skin and the moulding. Such a problem is almost non-existent if you shoot in an air-conditioned studio or in cold climates.

Of course, now we are helped out a lot with advances in VFX. VFX technicians can cover up the limitations in FX prosthesis. They can erase fault lines that may show between the skin and the prosthesis and blend the tone digitally to look even.

What are the effects of lights, HMI lights, on skin and how can make-up help?

VG: Good question. Because, beyond aesthetic reasons, there is another reason for make-up: to protect the actor's skin from harmful radiation, be it the sun's or of HMI lights. It's not possible that your skin will not be harmed if you act for hours day in and day out for months in the sun or in front of HMI lights, which attempt to duplicate natural light. That is why, in the old days, many senior actors suffered from black patches on their skin. Those days there was less awareness about exposure to strong lights and necessary precautions were not taken, and make-up was not that advanced as it is today.

Some actors come drunk on set or in a bad mood or frustrated with their lives or even upset about the film they are working on. How do you deal with such situations?

VG: We tend to overlook their personal issues. I can read their minds even before they sit on the make-up chair and surrender themselves to me. The make-up chair is the last chair the actor sits on before they visit the set for the take. The few hours or minutes they spend on this chair, it is my dharma to relax their mind in the time I have to execute their make-up. This is the primary responsibility of my profession. We must mentally relax the actor, help him reach the space or zone in his head that he needs to be in before walking on to the film set.

Some actors, in the middle of their make-up, without interrupting the process, will take me by surprise and ask me for advice. They seek advice on matters most personal and private. During such moments, I speak the truth, offer them advice from my heart. They may not act on my advice, but they listen. I know secrets about actors and actresses that I will take to my grave. They trust me and I will dishonour my profession by sharing those intimate secrets with even my God. I am certain there are others in my profession who can claim this too, in all humility. A make-up artist dabbles with far more than make-up and aesthetics.

What do you feel most proud about, beyond what you just narrated, which also humbles you?

VG: It is a tremendously humbling experience to have the trust of an actress who allows, after her mother who would dress her up and put make-up in her childhood, only her make-up artist to come close to her and apply make-up on her cheeks, lipstick or gloss on her lips.

How would you define what you do philosophically?

VG: A make-up artist is someone who can make you fall in love with your image and at the same time confront you with reality, if the need be. I can make you believe in the illusion needed for the film. Beyond that, I give you, an actor, a temporary face. A face that matches with some other soul. A soul that reflects the character you are playing. Once I give your character the face that belongs best to it, you as an actor can get on with doing a better job at playing that character.

If I asked you to do make-up for an artist, a person playing God, what kind of make-up would you do on that actor?

VG: I would do nothing. God needs no make-up. Because a child needs no make-up. And God is represented in the world of the living as a child. The only thing I would do is make his eyes look bigger than normal. Wide open, just like a child's, because they are so curious, a reflection of the innocent surprise at what they are viewing. Adults lose that curiosity as they grow up. That's why they lose their innocence. They begin to think they know so much and the curiosity and hunger to know more, learn more, experience more, die. But a child remains curious always, looking with so much interest at life. Just like God looks at his creations with so much interest and curiosity.

AUDIOGRAPHER, PRODUCTION SOUND MIXER, SOUND DESIGNER RAKESH RANJAN

Rakesh Bakshi: You have worked on nearly 180 films so far. In what capacity did you begin your professional journey?

Rakesh Ranjan (RR): I began as a production sound mixer and gradually worked my way up to a sound designer and director of audiography.

When did you first become aware of what sound recording in films really meant?

RR: Not until I joined FTII did I become aware of how sound is recorded in films. I joined FTII because I was interested in technology, especially electronics that had fascinated me since childhood, rather than sound. Having said that, the real attraction to sound was music, film songs.

Do you remember a sound from your childhood that is etched in your memory?

RR: That would probably be a sound I heard when I was visiting my village, Chakwai, now in Bihar, as a child. The village children would sneak into the sugarcane fields to steal sugarcane and the farmers, who owned the fields, would get alerted from

213

the 'khaskhaskhaskhaskhas' sound of the kids brushing past the over seven-foot-tall sugarcane stalks. That sound fascinated me. In a way, we could 'view' them through our ears! [*Laughs.*] If you know what I mean.

What is the normal brief you receive from a director when you come onboard a project?

RR: Rakesh, firstly, what surprises me is, most directors earlier did not give me/us audiographers, a script to read. That is unfortunate, because sound is such an integral part of the narrative, yet they don't think in terms of sound as a storytelling tool at all; for some, their storytelling is primarily actors and some interesting-looking location, well-choreographed songs and nice visuals. That's what they focus most of their creative energy on.

Having said that, the new generation of directors is very different. These directors are particular about their soundtrack, they share their thoughts with us from the preproduction stage itself. They also have a clear soundscape of the narrative.

What could be the reason that most directors pay more attention to visuals than sound, though sound forms 60 per cent of our senses?

RR: First, you have to understand that visually, cinema has evolved from 2D to 3D. But sound, well, it has evolved from mono to stereo, to immersive surround sound, which is 360 degrees spherical! So sound has added more dimensions than visual has. The elements of a film's soundtrack take you deeper into the narrative.

When you read a script, or when you discuss the sound treatment of the film, is there something you feel directors should include in the script or mention during their discussions with you?

RR: Yes, ideally, what they need to also write along with the dialogue and visual description of the shot is the soundscape, the aural space the scene is happening in and what the characters are hearing and reacting. All directors mention what they are seeing in their mind (visual perception of events) in relation to the story, but rarely do they include what they are hearing in their heads (aural perception of the story). They say, 'I see it my mind's eye,' but what about, 'I hear this in my head'? This is because they do not think of sound as an important tool in their narrative structure.

I have known of directors taking their cinematographer and their art director on recces but not their audiographers. Why is that so?

RR: Sadly, in India the director chooses a location because it suits him visually. They do not consult a production sound mixer/sound designer during outdoors recce. Once, one of my cinematographer friends complained to me about a senior audiographer onboard their film who wanted complete silence in and around the set or what we term 'sanitizing' the shooting location. But my pal did not realize that the director had chosen that location just for the look and not for the acoustical space or soundscape. In such a situation, the sound person, the production sound mixer, the audiographer, tries to capture primarily crystal-clear dialogue during the shoot. Dialogue being on the top of the hierarchy of storytelling, they try to 'sanitize' the location. Most committed directors select a location for the visual as well as the aural scape.

Production sound designer Simon Hayes was in India some years ago and he spoke about how much time and effort they put for the sound in the film *Les Miserables* (2012), how all the actors, art director, costume director, the cameraman and crew members helped him capture the original performances. Directors here, in India, give me a reference of the amazing sound quality in *Les Miserables* and other Hollywood films; however, if I attempt to make similar efforts, they think I am crazy! The kind of resources required to achieve that quality cannot be provided in terms of time and money. Many directors only pay lip service to good sound quality. They just talk about good sound because they are experiencing the magic of sound in Hollywood films and are in awe of that kind of sound experience, but sadly, that is where it ends. A typical sound post, a film's sound mix, which would normally take almost nine to twelve weeks to achieve in a Hollywood film, is executed in India in just two weeks! Producers kill it here by being in an extraordinary hurry to release their film, and in looking for 'deals' in the budget allotted to sound post-production.

Tell us about some important elements that you consider during production, so that you do not have problems with the sound during post-production. For example, how the fabric of the garments worn by actors or the materials the set is constructed or decorated with, etc., can affect you.

RR: There should be proper consideration for set construction and materials used. The actors' props are another important consideration and finally the acoustical space or the location where the set is being put up. The camera lights and gear should be silent, without any electrical disturbances.

Say, if you are shooting on a set constructed for a period film like, *Mughal-E-Azam* (1960), the set will be constructed of wood, the flooring will be of wood. But in real life, it was of stones, marble, etc., so the dialogue effects reflecting off these surfaces will naturally have a tonality of the setting materials, which is wood and not that of a highly reflecting surface marble.

As for clothes, sometimes the actors have to wear a particular kind of garment, which might be static-prone, so when we capture the dialogue on set or location, static noise can ruin the sound quality of the dialogue, because of which ADR becomes mandatory for those scenes.

Jewellery rustles is another aspect to be considered, because when the actors move about, it creates disturbances in the capture of the location sound. See, the recording mic spares none, it's the most truthful equipment and captures everything that strikes it; it is not biased; it is not selective. The above are the few elements we look out for in particular before principal photography begins, so that the producer and director have time on hand to implement any suggestions we may have.

So you would ideally like to be involved in the preproduction stage of the set building, location recce and costume designing?

RR: Absolutely! I think when one is telling a story, as in cinema, every member of the crew and cast can contribute aesthetically to the process, their input is very important, because they are experts in their own fields, so the earlier you can involve them in the process the better.

Is a sound designer also a storyteller? Do you create a theme for your sound treatment to enhance the narrative?

RR: Yes! The sound man is a very effective storyteller. He has to his disposal the various elements of the narrative—such as the dialogue, location ambiences, foleys, BGM and most importantly, silences—all of which constantly manipulate the audience's perception of the story along with the visuals and the visual edits.

I consider the sound textures as themes, because the tonal quality of all the sounds plays a very important part in the narrative, and this varies from subject to subject. I create sound texture by working on the tonal quality of the actor's voice, their footsteps, and other foley sounds. Other than that, what will be the sounds the audience will be hearing in the acoustical space of the story? That's what I create—what we term as 'soundscape'. What the audience hears, meaning, if it's an outdoor night scene, will people hear the crickets or an owl . . . which sound from the hundreds of options will help the narrative best is what I attempt to create as the film's sound designer. For me, this acoustical space is something very close to the story, because it subconsciously affects the perception of the audience and draws their attention to what the character is experiencing, feeling, hearing and reacting.

When you worked on Paan Singh Tomar (2012), *what kind of research did you do for creating the soundscape of the Chambal ravines?*

RR: One needs to travel to some regions to hear their particular and unique soundscapes; so I travelled to Chambal to work on the sound design of *Paan Singh*. Once there, I noticed the ravines are horizontal and vertical, so the wind makes a peculiar sound travelling through them. The sounds of the ravines during day and night were captured to use in the film during post. It was important that the audiences experience what Paan Singh was feeling or going through his journey with respect to the story's progression, and all sounds were placed in the narrative accordingly.

When you are dubbing dialogue during post-production, ADR, automated or additional dialogue replacement, what are you really looking for in the actor's voice?

RR: The texture, in context to the relationship, the expression of attitudes and emotions, or highlighting aspects of grammatical structure, keeping in mind the environment (the acoustical space), the spatial distances between the characters and objects around the person speaking, are some significant parameters.

The texture of the sound is my connectivity to the character and the narrative. I judge it by asking myself, while hearing the sound, the dialogue, if someone were to speak those words to me in those circumstances and environment, would I connect to them? So, I look for that answer, that texture. It is very difficult to explain texture, especially sound textures. It is a feeling I get when I hear something, be it dialogue, music or the effects or even silence!

Sound has a very strange quality that you are not aware of it unless it's muted. What is the importance of silence in a soundtrack?

RR: Many people feel muting something is silence. That is true, but I think about silence very differently. For me, silence is a close-up of sound. If I am creating silence on screen, I am drawing the attention of the audience to a narrative detail on screen. In the sense, say, if the director has shot just the eyes of the character, whatever be the magnification of the shot, and if I need to draw the attention of the audience to the emotion behind that close-up, I'll gradually create a vacuum of sound in the soundtrack, and I'd do it very subtly, to draw attention to a certain emotional experience. That's a close-up of sound for me, temporal silence, which I have created by changing the tonal characteristic. I'm not removing the sound completely, I'm not muting it, I'm only changing its tonal character.

Silence can be when you can hear the heartbeat of a person. Silence can be when you can hear distant sounds and associate them with your inner feelings.

Do you feel many Indian films have their background score at obnoxiously high levels?

RR: See, Rakesh, in many of our films, directors do not treat the background score as 'background' score, rather as foreground score! Also, the higher decibel levels at which they force us sound designers to maintain the background score has something to do with the screenplay or the story as well. The slow fade-in of the BGM is history, most often it comes as a bang and stays put at those high decibel levels.

When we tell some directors that the scene is working well without the score, they may not agree, maybe they are insecure with their material, and some will even boost the level and make it louder. Honestly, I feel they are not confident whether the scene is working without the background or not, so they feel they must take the help of the score to enhance the emotion, or maybe they do it to distract the audience from the poor writing or poor performance.

Your take on location sound versus dubbed (ADR) sound.

RR: Both have their advantages and disadvantages. For a film to have the final dialogue track captured on location, the script needs to be locked and in place much before the principal photography, the actors well-versed with their lines, with proper diction and feelings, the outdoor location should be enough to capture good and clean dialogue, the DOP, art director and costume designer should be sensitive to the requirements of the location sound mixer.

Above all, I think it is the attitude and discipline of the director and the crew members that matters the most in helping the location sound mixer do his job well and capture the original performance of the actors. The time and effort required to do a location-sound film is more than what it takes to just capture the guide audio track on location.

Whereas in case of a dubbed film, the sound crew can take it a bit easy on the shoot. Because their real work begins only after the film has been edited. The actors can concentrate and improve upon their performances. The tonal quality is totally under control as the actors are performing under ideal acoustical conditions.

Any other reason why many films have to resort to ADR, dubbing?

RR: There can be various factors from low budget to the actors not knowing the language.

As a sound designer, how important is a realistic sound to correct sound?

RR: Cinema sound cannot be realistic, it gives the perception of being real. That is because of the way we use sound to be projected in cinema halls. Realistic sound does not create cinematic impact. Created sound is more important than the realistic sound. What will go down well with the audience's perception is more important than the real sound.

For example, in *Ghayal* (1990), there is a sound of a knife stabbing a character. In reality, you may not even be able to hear the knife penetrating the human skin, because it may be a very soft 'tichhh' kind of sound. But because we needed the effect of the stabbing to be dramatic, I used multiple layers of sound effects—like the tearing of a thin cloth, a knife stabbing a big chunk of meat and being pulled out, a few fresh tomatoes being squashed, the sound of a punch, and a sharp metallic ring 'tunngggg'—to create that one single stabbing sound you heard in the film.

As a sound designer, what do you really bring to a director, other than effects, levels, clarity of audio, etc.? What do you think is your real job underlying these tasks?

RR: I think my main job is to communicate and enhance the audiences' experience/perception of the story.

Considering most of our films are heavy on sound, tell us, how much can an audience really hear that will be useful, because I feel most film-makers overwhelm an audience with sound.

RR: Sound is very complex, Rakesh. And putting together a soundtrack is even more complex. There is a fact about our brain that directors and music composers must know. It is known as 'selective' hearing. The ears are not where we hear sound actually; they are simply the funnel that carries sound waves to our brain. The real 'hearing'/perception of the sounds happens in our brain. Many sounds strike our ears and even make their way to our brain; however, the brain is selective and mutes some sounds and enhances others.

The brain will select the sounds in context to what our PoV is, what our need is at that moment. It filters out and blocks all other sounds that are unnecessary to us at that moment in time. So as a sound designer, you have to be selective, just like the human brain. You have to think, 'What is most important among all the information being received in a shot?' and filter or mute the rest, and thus drive/focus the audience's perception to what is important in that shot and help the narrative.

How would you really define your job, your profession?

RR: I'm a psychiatrist, a sound psychiatrist, if such a term can be coined. I play constantly with the perception of the audience in cinema hall; I simply manipulate human perception to achieve an enhanced feeling towards the narrative.

Can you elaborate on the selective hearing of the brain and why it is important for a director and music composer?

RR: Suppose you have three loud sounds happening at one moment and you create a fourth loud sound. Not only will the fourth loud sound not be perceived by the brain but the first three will also become less effective.

I'll give you an example. Music directors of the'70s or even earlier would compose the orchestra with minimal loud sounds amongst the many instruments playing simultaneously. They would enhance only three main sounds, instruments and keep others at lower levels. If I sing a song from the '50s or the '60s, I will be able to give you the interlude music and even sing the tabla–dholki sounds. Whereas, if you take a song nowadays, I doubt I can sing any of the interludes. That is because, all the instruments are playing as loud as each other, so they all become less effective. The brain doesn't even notice, register, any loud sounds beyond three or four and perceives the rest as noise and filters them out.

To give you an example of good sound engineering, music composer A.R. Rahman composes many tracks but during the final mix begins to shut them one by one until he reaches a point where he feels what is important has remained open. Hear his compositions, they are so neat, crystal clear.

If you were to create the sound of God speaking for a character playing God, what would you do to make them sound godly?

RR: I will create a voice which is passionate, soft and at the same time warm. When you say God, all the passion, all the love, all the kindness, all the good things come to mind, and that is what God represents. So the voice I create will have to reflect that kind of tonal quality. That's it! The voice should make you feel at peace within.

Something you want to add, share with us before we end this interview?

RR: I would like to quote Satyajit Ray. When he was asked, 'How do you tell a story? What are the things you keep in mind when you are telling a story?' he replied, 'When, as a child, my grandparents would tell me a story, I now recollect how I would be engaged by their stories. It was just someone telling me a story verbally, no support of visuals and music, yet I would be hooked. Even though it was just an audio track playing, them telling me the story, the kind of interest they created in me to listen to them keenly, by modulating their voices, changing the pitch and tonal quality in context to the changes in drama being narrated, that kept me hooked to their storytelling. That is it! And they told the stories simply, they were not loud, yet I can remember them even today!'

Reading this I realized, just like a woman does not need jewellery to look beautiful, if your story is good, you do not need to decorate it with loud or unnecessary sounds. Keep it simple.

ACKNOWLEDGEMENTS

To begin with, a massive THANK YOU to all those who still make me believe I am a better writer and a better person than I really am.

One of the reasons I became an author was to remain relevant for some special people in my life, including myself; to give my life meaning and purpose when I could not make a feature film of my own over a period of ten years. Volume 1 of *Directors' Diaries*, published in 2015, was my first book. Stories are all around us. We all have a story to tell, and, perhaps, there is a book or a film or a painting in all of us. However, few are lucky or blessed enough to be able to put their thoughts on pages that others will read.

My heartfelt gratitude to many generous and affectionate people. I've asked so many for all kinds of help. So many people have helped me reach wherever I am today. No one can do it alone. Our life is one big adventure, with many heroes and heroines. We are never the sole protagonists of our story. Innumerable people over the years have given me kindness, inspiration, insight and love.

So, I am grateful to my parents, my brother Rajesh, my sisters Suman and Kavita, and their families, Nidhi, Rohit, Sunny, Chandni, Kahil, Divya, Karan, Shreya, Sidhant, Vinay and Sanju, and my extended family—close friends, particularly Rohit and Ambiii. Our lives would be incomplete without us paying regular gratitude for the rituals of good friendships and companionships that add meaning and purpose to our lives. Thank you for being my friends, Satya, Ritu, Shomieee, Maneck, Laila, Dilnaz, Dinyar,

Tony, Anupama, Sonu, Priyanka, Meghna, Benaifer, Khusrav, Siddhi, Kanika, Akira, Priyanka, Advait, Neelam, Abhay, Rishi, Shashi, Pooja, Changez, Mayura, Vivek, Ankita, Himanshu, Manoj, Mukesh, Varsha, Akshita, Nishil, Fatty, Sydney, Dr Apte, Amin, Charlotte, Shachi, Dr Ishani, Ekta, Samiere, Bobby, Amit, Rohan, Vidyun, Tony, Meenu, Swami, Sushrut, Bhavesh, Rustom, Kalpa, Raghu, Paramjit, Arvind, Babbu ji, Vimala and Papa's Girl Shweta.

Thanks to my transcriber Priya Sindher aka Toofan Mail. Without her speed, I would not have been able to edit the transcripts within a few weeks of the interviews. I must also thank Devika Chibber and Hetal Varia for the transcriptions they executed so well for our book.

Thanks to Meghna Ghai Puri and Rahul Puri for access to the immense library of books and films at Whistling Woods International Institute of Film, Communication and Creative Arts, Mumbai, for my research needs. Meghna also introduced me to two brilliant students, who read the edited conversations in the first draft of my manuscript and gave me their feedback—Ritambhara Dixit and Vidushi Goel were sharp, critical and, most importantly, enthusiastic and cheerful to work with. Thank you, Subhash Ghai, for the preface of our book.

The first volume of this book was also a tribute to the world's first full-length feature film, *The Story of the Kelly Gang* (1906), directed by Charles Tait, and to *Raja Harishchandra* (1913), directed by Dadasaheb Phalke, the first feature film made in India. We, the publisher and I, decided to add one more significant contributor to that tribute to the earliest known film-makers: Saraswati Phalke. Saraswati bai, maiden name Kaveribai Karandikar, wife of Dadasaheb, was the editor on her husband's film, making her India's first film editor! We both wished to highlight Saraswati bai's contribution to film-making in India here.

Thanks to Penguin Random House India's executive editor Shantanu Ray Chaudhuri and commissioning editor

Gurveen Chadha for reviewing my thoughts, and revising and coordinating my manuscript to a published book.

A massive thanks to *Reader's Digest*—a wholesome magazine that inspired my father, and subsequently me for nearly half my lifetime—and actor Ingrid Bergman. I read her biography in 2002 and it reaffirmed my passion and love for biographies, writing, film-making and movies. Thanks also to the wonderful Internet and its vast resources. What would our lives be without them! Thanks to printed books, we can hold them so close to our hearts while we peep into their worlds within. How many people do we allow to come so close?

Stay curious, stay inspired, stay loved, stay kind.

PHOTO CREDITS FOR
COVER IMAGES

Abhishek Chaubey picture courtesy Pratik Karwade
Kabir Khan picture courtesy Zaheer Abbas
Mohit Suri picture courtesy Venu Rasuri
Nandita Das picture courtesy Nandita Das
Prabhu Deva picture courtesy Mohan Komati (Popmercy)
Shakun Batra picture courtesy Shakun Batra
Shyam Benegal picture courtesy Shyam Benegal
Tanuja Chandra picture courtesy Tejinder Singh at the Mumbai
    Film Festival